Plan to Party

Plan to Party

*Simple & Special Entertaining
In Your Home*

**By Elizabeth Mascali and Dawn Sandomeno
of Partybluprints**

FOREWORD BY JEANNE BENEDICT

Published by Yorkshire Publishing
9731 East 54th Street
Tulsa, OK 74146
www.yorkshirepublishing.com

YorkshirePublishing
www.yorkshirepublishing.com
Write Now.

Editor | Caroline Webster
Cover Design and Interior Page Design | Julie Curtis Design
Image Production | Steve Walkowiak
Assistant Designer | Vicki Frye, Typography Creations
Illustrations and Icons | Sol Linero
Proofreader | Laura Matthews

Photography Credits by Page:

Alexandra Mascali; Pgs. 33, 40, 50, 76, 109, 125, 147, 149, 150, 163, 166, 183,
192, 209, 211, 237, 241, 242, 245, 246, 249, 251, 253, 257, back cover

Elizabeth Mascali; Cover, Pgs. 7, 36, 43, 46, 54, 78, 80, 81, 86, 90, 95, 96, 103,
109, 111, 112, 135, 140, 144, 152, 154, 164, 167, 169, 181, 195, 196, 197, 199, 200, 203,
206, 209, 212, 238, 257, 260, back cover

Dawn Sandomeno; Pg. 53

Briana E. Heard/be heard photography; Pgs. 11, 16, 20, 28, 62, 121, back cover headshot

All others: istockphoto.com or dreamstime.com

ISBN: 978-0-88144-218-2

Printed in Canada by Friesens Corporation.

Acknowledgments

From Elizabeth

To my family, Arnie, Ally, and Jack, for their unending understanding, patience, support and "resourcefulness" throughout this process. Their unselfish attitude let me focus and dedicate the time, effort, and resources to do something I always wanted to do—publish a book. They helped my dream come true.

To my husband, the best writer I know, you are my compass, counsel, and cornerstone (my true partner in every way). You inspire me every day in countless ways, and I could not have done this without you.

To Dawn, my partner and dear friend, your faith and confidence in me allowed us to venture down this exciting path. As always, working on this with you enriched the experience—what an adventure!

To my parents for raising me to believe I could do anything and for always supporting and encouraging me. To my entire family for their love and support and for always being ready for a party!

And to all my friends for their caring, enthusiasm, and support.

From Dawn

To my partner and amazing husband Mark, thanks for always trusting and believing there was something to this and loving me unconditionally. Thanks to my three beautiful boys, Nicholas, Jake, and Mark, who cheered me on, teased me, prayed for me, and each day are my biggest supporters!

To my mother, sisters Donna and Heather, and my in-laws Laura and Paul. I am grateful for all your love, support, and encouragement.

A special thanks to my dearest friends, who always respond to the call for help: Pam, Kelly, Missy, Hoops, Mary, Christie, and Sheila.

And of course to Elizabeth, whose courage, confidence and "yin" to my "yang" made the journey to this point fun. I owe you all a party!

From the Partybluprints Girls

Thanks to Yorkshire Publishing and Todd Rutherford for doing what had to be done to get this book published, and to Todd for his friendship.

Special thanks to Alexandra Mascali who contributed to this book by performing countless jobs in addition to being a featured photographer.

Thanks to those who believed in us and supported us from the beginning. Special thanks to Brian Massey for lending his talent in music and design to our brand and creating our fabulous logo, and Rich Adams, www.pathosstudios.com, for his brilliant design work. Very special thanks to our Resident Wine Expert, Kirk Sprenger (www.chappaquawine.com)—there's always a party when Kirk's in the house. Also thanks to Bryan Azorsky for design and technical expertise in creating "Book Links" on our blog.

Thanks to Pamela Pinta for marketing and design advice since the inception of Party Bluprints, Inc. Her friendship and talent are treasured.

Thanks to Christie Everling for PR in the launch phase of Party Bluprints, Inc.

Thanks to Beth Feldman, founder of RoleMommy.com and BeyondPR, and Katja Presnal, founder SkimbacoLifestyle.com and creator of the Skimbaco Lifestyle Brand, for opening many doors.

Table of Contents

*Partybluprints Feature: Specially selected posts from the Partybluprints blog, www.partybluprintsblog.com.

62 SECTION III: PARTY PLANS

PARTY PLANS

Foreword

BY JEANNE BENEDICT

EVER GO TO A PARTY, not really knowing any one, and then instantly hit it off with a person? You think, "Wow, we could be friends for life!" That's how I feel about Dawn and Elizabeth. Funny thing is… we met online in the world of parties, and it was a mutual passion for celebrating, respect for each others' ideas, and I have to say, a mom-vibe that you get from like-minded women you want to hang out with after dropping off the kids at school, that made me fall in love with these gals!

Partybluprints: Plan to Party is brilliant. With this book, the authors have made hanging out in style a whole lot easier and less stressful for the party host by sharing tips, tricks, and detailed step-by-step guides for throwing four incredible parties from start to finish.

But, what I like most about Dawn and Elizabeth is that they've "got your back" through the whole party planning process. Sure, they have fabulous ideas that will make your event a success, but more importantly, they really care about the time and money that you're going to invest in a party and truly want the very best experience for you and your guests.

In fact, you should think of them as your party BFFs (Best Friends Forever). They're the girls who are invited guests at a get-together in your home and graciously say, "Do you need any help?" Then, they really do help you, from picking up empty glasses to answering the door when you're busy in the kitchen, welcoming another guest on your behalf. They've translated that generosity, talent, and "nuts and bolts" entertaining smarts into this book that will help you throw a great event whether you're a first time host or a home party pro.

I've been in the party arena for a long time, from writing four books myself, to hosting a TV theme party show, *Weekend Entertaining,* on the DIY Network, to making over 100 appearances as a party expert and chef on shows like the *Today Show, Live with Regis and Kelly*, and *The Ellen Degeneres Show*. But my daily career in the online and social media world interacting with fellow entertaining experts and bloggers like Dawn and Elizabeth is the real-life connectivity that builds inspiration for all the work that we love to do; you could say it's a life bluprint.

This foreword is more than an introduction to these these wonderful women; it's a toast to friendship— my friendship with Dawn and Elizabeth and your friendships spent in celebration at the parties and occasions that make up those moments we call life!

—Jeanne Benedict,
Cookbook and Lifestyle Author and Party Expert
www.jeannebenedict.com

It takes hands to build
a house, but only hearts
can build a home.

—Author Unknown

About Us

The Partybluprints Girls

THE PARTY WITHIN US

ELIZABETH MASCALI

I've learned that people will forget what you said, people will forget what you did, but people will never forget how you made them feel.

—Maya Angelou

WHEN I TAKE A MOMENT to think about why I love to entertain, the answer is simple. Parties connect me with my family and friends. We have been blessed with many occasions to celebrate in our home: births, baptisms, birthdays, anniversaries, communions, holidays, friendships, and simply having one another. We all love a good party, but most of all we love being together. We lead busy lives, and these occasions give us an excuse to take a break from the outside world and reconnect. I treasure these moments, and I know my children, family, and friends do, too. Such moments continue to connect us when we return to our daily lives.

While my entertaining style has evolved over the years, I did follow a noticeable pattern. I always tried to go all out, taking a lot of time to plan, prepare, and seek out special touches because I wanted everything to be perfect (really special). The party was my opportunity to create a memorable time for my guests (my gift to them), and I wanted it to be extraordinary. However, this drive for perfection began taking a toll on my entertaining experience. Over time, I realized I needed to redefine my concept of the perfect party. So, with a bit more focus and reflection, and a renewed vigor, I began my quest to reconnect with the purpose of my entertaining and develop a smarter approach that fit my lifestyle. By developing strategies, tools, resources, and plans to entertain, I discovered a new comfort and confidence level. Entertaining became more enjoyable, and the best part was that I did not need to work any harder, just smarter.

I now know that I am at my best as a host when I relax my pursuit of perfection and allow myself to roll with the party rhythm, a rhythm choreographed initially by me but dictated ultimately by my guests. The meter of that party rhythm is rarely uninterrupted, so I've incorporated some important strategies while entertaining: flexibility and humor. Sometimes the fun comes when things do not go as planned.

A perfect example was my son's First Holy Communion party. We invited seventy-five of our closest friends and family members to our home to celebrate the occasion. It was a beautiful day, and everyone was in and out of the house. Kids were playing, and the adults were eating, drinking, laughing, and genuinely enjoying themselves. I allowed myself a moment to take in this "Rockwell" scene, proud of the moment. The peaceful scene in my head shattered when I heard several of my guests start yelling all at once. Looking for the source of the "excitement," I turned and saw that the tablecloth on one of the buffet tables was on fire! With the assistance of one of my nephews (who, as it turns out, accidently set the fire while lighting the Sternos—no, I've never let him forget it), we extinguished the fire, turned the tablecloth around to hide the charred hole in the cloth, and did not miss but two beats of the party. No one was the wiser, those involved all had a good laugh, and the rhythm of the party continued.

Throughout my childhood and into adulthood, there have been (and continue to be) "inspirational" hosts who are responsible for "entertaining"

in the family. I have been blessed with the opportunity to take from each of them something special, and it's my desire to pass it on.

My mother, Karen, taught me all the basics and a little more on everything I needed to know about cooking, baking, caring for and preparing a warm home, and, perhaps most importantly, how to make guests feel welcomed and loved. From extraordinary family gatherings on holidays and birthdays, to weekend parties with friends, to just celebrating being together, my mother has always worn a loving smile with eyes beaming—joyful that we were together and so happy to be able to treat us to a special gathering. Her genuine warmth touches all in her presence, and it is always an honor and true pleasure to be invited into her home.

I remember as a child how glamorous the Saturday night parties she would host with my father, Richard, seemed to me and my brother, Rich. My mother spent the days preceding the party cooking, cleaning, setting the table just right, creating intricate appetizers and exquisite dishes, and baking desserts from scratch. On these special Saturday nights, my mother served us an early dinner and saw that we were bathed and in our pajamas before the guests arrived. These parties were adults only, and we needed no reminder to stay quiet and out of sight. I remember sitting at the top step of the stairs with my brother, listening as the guests arrived, imagining myself as host one day. Greetings were exchanged and mood music filled the air, as my father mixed cocktails and my mother served food and "warmed up" the crowd. I still treasure the memories of the sounds of those evenings, and even today I can almost hear the harmonious laughter from the guests downstairs—with my mother directing the chorus.

When I started my own family, our family celebrations were always special, but definitely on the smaller, more intimate side. I gained an entirely new perspective on entertaining when I met my husband's family. When Arnie invited me to Christmas Eve, I was filled with nervous excitement; this would be my introduction to his family. His immediate family of twenty people had already started the party when I arrived— eating, drinking, and laughing. I did not know that this was all a precursor to the dancing that would break out at some point during every party. The spirit was unlike anything I had ever experienced. Talk about living in the moment. This was the first of many gatherings, celebrations, and parties we would share. As our extended family grows, there is always something to celebrate and we're always up for a party.

With a family so large, only an organized, talented, and experienced hostess could orchestrate our parties. That role has been handled deftly by my mother-in-law, Cathy, another role model of mine. To this day, I still marvel at how she delights in welcoming everyone into her home and to her table, meal after meal, holiday after holiday, and celebration after celebration. I learned from my mother-in-law how to relax and enjoy being surrounded by loved ones—and how to feed a crowd! Cathy, like my mom, takes great joy in hosting and feeding her family, and she too is a master at making her guests feel special, even when there are dozens at the party.

These "inspirational" hosts made me feel special every time I was in their home. Whether it was a full-blown event or a simple dinner, there was always at least one touch and a look that said, "I thought of you and wanted to make you feel special and loved." I carry that sentiment forward.

While my entertaining style has developed over the years, I have had the benefit of an inspirational co-host, my husband, Arnie. His warm, fun, and generous spirit fills a room whenever we entertain. From our first party together to present day, Arnie has the innate ability to warm up any room and "entertain" our guests simply by living in the moment—talk about creating a party rhythm. The greatest "entertaining" lesson I have learned from him is how a host can set the tone. He is a constant example of how much love, fun, and good spirit can be created and shared under one roof. I love co-hosting a party with him, beginning to end, and I love how our party continues after the guests have left and we recap the fun had by all. This excitement has carried over into Partybluprints, as my family's support has turned into interest and involvement. Party planning has become a part of our family's life (they love the research and development behind each plan).

My last "shout-out" goes to my business partner, dear friend and frequent co-host, Dawn. I am so fortunate to have the opportunity to work at what I love and Dawn is a big reason why. Building Partybluprints with a partner who is the "yang" to my "yin" (when we started the business I was the "yang" and she the "yin"—funny how the energy effortlessly transfers between us, always remaining a whole) has allowed me and our company to grow tremendously. Over the course of more than thirteen years, Dawn and I developed a friendship based on trust, respect, and loyalty that was a

natural source of confidence when making the decision to work together to build Partybluprints. We each knew each other's strengths and weaknesses and were confident that our collective skill set was a perfect fit. Although I enjoy many aspects of the business, our collaborative efforts when designing parties is a highlight—our minds and hands working in sync to create an experience to be enjoyed by many.

As you venture with us behind the scenes at Partybluprints, take a moment to reflect on any gatherings with family and friends in your own life that inspired and touched you in some way. Open yourself up to discovery as you read our tried-and-true "bluprints" for success. I'm so excited to share our "insider's secrets" (strategies, techniques, and tools) along with some of our favorite Party Plans.

Well-hosted parties give people a chance to slow down, re-connect, and create memories that add grace, beauty, and humor to our lives. A good party never ends. The memories last a lifetime—and longer.

I hope you will be inspired to celebrate life in your home joyfully and often.

Cheers!

Elizabeth

Elizabeth Loves...

Favorite Party Plan: Wine Country Crush.

Fantasy party: Outdoor Wine Pairing Dinner in Napa Winery—featuring all local food and wine.

Who I would invite: My husband and I would host our family and dear friends.

Best party I have hosted: My wedding. The spirit at this party was infectious—joyful family and friends, ecstatic bride and groom, and insanely fun dancing (we all danced the entire evening). Truly, a great celebration of life for all.

What made it special: One of my happiest moments was marrying my husband, Arnie. Our two families came together in joyful celebration to mark our union. This day connected our families and marked the beginning of the family we would create together.

Single best party advice: Be prepared!

Best party trick: Buy votive candles and holders in bulk and light them throughout the house. They provide a huge impact for a small investment. Candlelight makes everyone and everything look good, sets a warm tone, and hides a multitude of imperfections.

Favorite party music: I like a variety of "party music." Music is a must at any party, but my favorite is dependent on the vibe of the party. I love our music mix from the Chocolate Soiree Party Plan. Every time I hear a song from that mix, it reminds me of an incredibly fun night!

Favorite cocktail: French 75, and it always tastes better when I enjoy it with my friends. (Thank you Karen and Margaret for introducing me to this special cocktail). I, of course, shared the discovery with Dawn—it only took her one sip to love it.

Favorite food: Risotto with fresh vegetables served with a glass of Napa Cabernet.

Favorite color: Partybluprints "blu," of course.

Favorite flower: Peony.

Favorite cake: Birthday cake—any type. I love the tradition surrounding the presentation of the cake. My father-in-law has perfected the birthday cake "processional" by exaggerating the time to blow out the candles. His version extends the time it should take to count "1, 2, 3!" building the anticipation for all. This tradition has been part of the family for generations.

The Partybluprints Girls

THE PARTY WITHIN US

DAWN SANDOMENO

To persuade a friend to stay for lunch is a triumph and a precious honour.
To entertain many together is to honor them all mutually.
It is equally an honour to be a guest.
—*Claudia Roden, food writer "A Book of Middle Eastern Food" (1968)*

....

MY LOVE OF PARTIES STARTED EARLY. I remember sitting in my kitchen listening to the adults downstairs at the parties my parents hosted. If parties were the light, then I was a moth to the flame. To this day, my passion for parties has never waned. I did not grow up in a large home, but it was still well-equipped for parties. A basement bar, a small pool outside, and a large dining room table were the foundations of all our parties. My childhood home is where my image of "simple and special" was formed; my parents were masters at it.

My father always created the right vibe for a party with his attention to details like lighting, music, and fun activities. Barbeques always included outdoor music, a game of croquet set up on the lawn, and, when it got dark, my father would string lanterns by the patio and light tiki torches. You can imagine how magical this was to my sisters and me. To this day, I try to evoke that feeling in guests at my parties, and I love to make children in attendance feel that they are special and an important part of the day.

My father was also a passionate gardener and grew enough vegetables each summer to feed our family and most of the neighbors. My mother would can the extras for winter. Being exposed to lots of fresh food as a kid made me appreciate what fresh ingredients can bring to a meal and how they can enrich a recipe.

My mother had her own party spirit and it filled our home with warmth. With her good humor and easy manner, she was a great hostess and made everyone feel special. She went along with my father's party plans and executed them perfectly—all with three kids in tow! She always hosted holidays with a traditional sit-down dinner, and the images, smells, and tastes are vivid memories that still bring me great joy today. My sisters and I were always inviting friends to our home, and, as we got older, we would bring friends home from college to stay for days or even a week. It was because of the way my mother made each one of them feel that they always wanted to come back. She opened her heart, made everyone feel comfortable, and kept a special drawer of sweets in our house that was always a guest favorite! Things were never fancy; they were simple and special. My mother always gave guests her time and attention. Friends who came to our house loved spending their alone time with my mother. She taught me this great lesson in entertaining—you should always be present at your own party. I am still trying to master this one.

I grew up and married my amazing husband, Mark. I found a partner who enjoyed having people into our home as much as I did. Mark is a wonderful bartender and a master at music. He is a great co-host at the parties we throw at home, and if we are hosting a tailgate or picnic, he is in charge. We work like a well-oiled machine when preparing for guests. We love to host the holidays for our families and BBQs at the beach for friends. Mark introduced me to a new style of entertaining by bringing my beautiful mother-in-law

and father-in-law into my life. Comfortable hosting a crowd, these two welcome everyone and anyone with big open hearts. My mother-in-law, a magnificent cook, could put out fifty pounds of corned beef (not kidding) at Saint Patrick's Day or eight pounds of linguine for Christmas Eve dinner and still serve dessert with a smile on her face. There is no one I know who takes greater pleasure in giving pleasure through the food on her table. My father-in-law is so sincere in his appreciation of having his wife, children, and grandchildren at his table, it gives him a tear in his eye as he toasts each of us every holiday.

As I developed my own style of entertaining, I tried to marry these two approaches to hosting parties and crea te a formula that worked for me. My evolution as a hostess started with many stumbles and a few falls. After a few years, I got it right, at least most of the time, and, with my dear friend Elizabeth, focused on creating plans that others could follow.

I love to plan parties! To this day, I cannot pass up an offer to plan one or help someone else plan one. I have been hosting parties in my own home for more than sixteen years, including holidays and special occasions both large and small. These were first hosted in a tiny apartment and now take place in our home in New Jersey and at the beach.

Outside the home, I have planned charity galas for more than ten years. I take great pleasure in these events and consider them a tribute to my father and his party spirit. He passed away after a long and brave battle with cancer in 1995. I have also planned events for numbers in the hundreds, such as sports banquets, school carnivals, women's only dining and shopping events, as well as parties for friends and family members in their homes.

My wish is that my love for parties will inspire you to entertain and that the experience and expertise I have gained over the years will make it as easy and fun for you as it is for me.

Cheers!

Dawn

Dawn Loves...

Favorite Party Plan: Chocolate Soiree.

Fantasy party: A destination party in a villa on the Almafi coast in Italy that would last for days.

Who I would invite: My family and closest friends.

Best party I have ever hosted: My wedding—one of the happiest days of my life and a great party; ask anyone who was there!

What made it special: The love in the room that overflowed from Mark and me, and our family and friends—and perhaps knowing down deep that it was my father's last party. We cherished every moment.

Single best party advice: Know your guests, and make your party a reflection of you, not the latest trend.

Best party trick: Pick a make-ahead menu, and be present at your own party.

Favorite party music: An eclectic mix or any mix my husband makes—he creates the best party mixes.

Favorite cocktail: French 75, thanks Elizabeth!

Favorite food: Any kind of pasta.

Favorite color: Blue.

Favorite flower: Gerbera Daisy.

Favorite cake: Dark-Chocolate Cake with Ganache Frosting

THE CREATION
OF PARTYBLUPRINTS

PARTIES AND GATHERINGS WEAVE OUR LIVES
together with those we love. We found that as life
grew more hectic and demanding, entertaining was
slowly became another item on the to-do list. We set
out to eliminate the factors that detracted from the
true joy of entertaining, while enhancing the overall
party experience.

Via traveling, researching, cooking, and analyzing
all of the components in planning and hosting parties,
we discovered what we were looking for: a fresh,
simple, and special way to entertain in our homes. In
an attempt to share this unique style of entertaining,
we built Partybluprints Party Plans. Despite our busy
and demanding schedules, these Party Plans allow us
to enjoy our guests and our parties.

Elizabeth and Dawn in the Whitehall Lane Vineyards. This trip fueled our love affair with food and wine and inspired our Wine Country Crush Party Plan.

In April 2007, we founded Party Bluprints, Inc., and launched www.partybluprints.com that fall and, shortly thereafter, The Partybluprints Blog, www.partybluprintsblog.com, with the goal of building an invaluable resource for enjoyable entertaining at home.

Our journey in building Partybluprints has been fun, exciting, and, at times, challenging. However, our work does have inherent benefits—we really enjoy the research and development. We comb the country, including our local area, to taste, feel, listen, look, and, yes, sniff out what's best, whether it's a new dish, drink, or the next hot product. Everywhere we go, everything we experience, could lead to our next big find and is a potential Partybluprints inspiration. We are always looking for our next great adventure, discovery, or inspiration, so join our party and be our guest at The Partybluprints Blog, www.partybluprintsblog.com. We'd love to hear what you think!

We've shared great meals and had experiences too vast and varied to name in entirety here, all while feeding our passion for food, wine, and travel. No one thing stands out, but a memory of all our senses being triggered in some magical way, bringing us to a place we'll always remember. Of our favorite experiences, there's a common thread—we've been made to feel welcomed, relaxed, and inspired. Through Partybluprints, we bring these experiences and this sentiment, to your table. We've done the legwork so that you can enjoy the rewards.

The Partybluprints Philosophy

WE BELIEVE that entertaining in your home can enrich your life. The goal of Partybluprints is to inspire home entertaining that nurtures personal connections.

We are committed to designing high-quality Party Plans that make entertaining simple and special.

Life is truly good …

Share it with others …

Open the possibilities for Extraordinary Entertaining.

Light the Way …

L	I	G	H	T
live	inspire	give	hope	thrive

BIRTHDAY WISHES

*And in the end, it's not the years in your life that count.
It's the life in your years.*
—*Abraham Lincoln*

I HAVE ALWAYS LOVED birthday celebrations (for others, more than my own). It is one day devoted to celebrating a human being's presence in this world. We'll never know or appreciate how much one person's words, actions, or presence affect others (we are not all *It's a Wonderful Life*'s George Bailey), but I do believe we are all intertwined. Whether you give a small kindness (a smile, encouraging word or simple gesture) or gifts that keep on giving (time, loyal friendship, compassion, love), give as often as you can. It's a great way to celebrate your birth all year long.

This year, make sure you view your birthday as your friend, not your enemy. Embrace it and celebrate it in a new and special way to mark the day this world changed because you entered it.

*Birthdays are good for you.
Statistics show that the people who have the most live the longest.*
—*Larry Lorenzoni*

My birthday wish is that my "light" continues to grow stronger and shine brighter than ever, and that I can positively touch others, fanning their flame as well. Thank you to all the special people who have nurtured my light this past year. I will pass it on.

Dawn and I are grateful for all of you, your time, support and good wishes. I am blessed to share, not only a birthday week with Dawn, but a business, daily life, friendship, and deep respect. I believe our light shines brighter because of the balance of the yin and yang—our hope is to share this light with others.

Cheers to celebrating your birth every day of the year!

Elizabeth

Our Wish

A special message from Elizabeth

AS MENTIONED EARLIER, celebrating life with family and friends was always an important part of my family's life. It is obvious that I recognize the importance of entertaining, having designed an entire approach and company to inspire and empower others to entertain. Although I did not need a wakeup call to appreciate the importance of spending time with friends and family, I received one in 2009. Diagnosed with breast cancer and facing nine months of treatment, I was "sidelined" for the better part of a year, fighting on the front line, all my resources dedicated solely to one thing—doing whatever I had to do to beat this disease. With the unwavering support of my husband, family, and friends, I beat the cancer. It was a challenging journey, but I emerged in 2010 with a vengeance, recommitted to how important spending time with family and friends is and to sharing that message in this book.

At this crucial crossroad, Dawn promised me, "I'll make sure there's something for you to come back to." Dawn worked tirelessly at great sacrifice to keep her promise. I cannot thank her enough. We were strong through this crisis that faced us separately, personally, and professionally, and together we are a committed and passionate force. Never willing to stay on the sidelines watching, we are looking to squeeze every moment out of every day and every experience. We are both recommitted to being a valuable resource to facilitate people connecting—what better place to do it than in your home?

Partybluprints is a home the two of us built from the ground up with passion, determination and a commitment to quality. We are thrilled you accepted our invitation into our homes by reading our book. Our hope is that we earn your trust, respect, and loyalty and that we might vicariously enter your home whenever you host a party, whether you reference our tried-and-true "bluprints" for success and create your own plan or follow our plans to a tee.

Thank you for visiting and taking the time to get to know us a bit. We hope you visit us often whether it is through this book or online and that you make a point to celebrate life as often as you can.

Partybluprints Basics

PARTYBLUPRINTS WAS CREATED to revolutionize the way you entertain. "Simple and special" is our mantra. Our objective is to inspire you to entertain in a unique way. We want to:

1. ENCOURAGE YOU to entertain by providing you with ideas and inspirations;

2. EQUIP YOU with strategies, techniques, tools, and plans to build your own party;

3. ENABLE YOU to execute strategies and plans based on your available resources; and

4. EMPOWER YOU by laying the foundation for you to succeed.

Our unique style of entertaining focuses on the overall party experience for both the guests and the host (we'll let you in on our secrets in our "Essence of Entertaining"). Planning a party is a skill to be developed and honed, and the best way to do that is to follow a tried-and-true method.

Enter Partybluprints. After extensive research, design, development, and, yes, partying (we have to test them out), we deliver to you fully-coordinated, comprehensive, and step-by-step Party Plans. Party Plans are your "bluprint" for success to make entertaining in your home extraordinary.

Section Three contains four Party Plans, which guide you from beginning to end in planning, preparing and hosting a party. But, before we get there, this section shares our favorite entertaining secrets and strategies to strengthen your entertaining toolbox, all the while encouraging and empowering you to build fun and fabulous parties.

Before we get started, consider this: if you wanted to build a house, would you do it without a proper plan, tools, and "know-how," and still expect the results to be good? This book provides an approach to entertaining that allows you to build a great party for you and your guests (yes, you can be a guest at your own party). Remember, our goal is to inspire home entertaining that nurtures personal connections. So, get ready to see how revolutionizing the way you approach entertaining is a way to enrich your life.

Essence of Entertaining

WE BELIEVE THE PERFECT PARTY EXPERIENCE is achieved when people simply feel good, relaxed, and open to connecting with others. Follow these important tips, and free your guests' senses for a fabulous and memorable experience.

* Entertain not to impress, but to address, and enjoy your guests. Entertaining in your home is an opportunity to treat your friends and family to a special and personal experience—treat it as such.
* Devise a plan to manage your time and tasks so you are not overwhelmed or unprepared for your guests. If you plan carefully, you can prepare everything ahead of time and be a guest at your own party.
* We believe the most effective (and fun) way to approach entertaining is to start with a plan to stimulate the five senses. Pay attention to all the elements of your party and make sure they enhance, and do not detract from, each other (consider it a symphony for the senses): the food, the tablescape, the music, the lighting, etc. If you achieve the right balance, your guests' senses will be satisfied, resulting in relaxed and happy guests and the perfect party environment!

To help you address your guests and their senses, here are some "good sense" tips to stimulate the five senses when entertaining:

* **Palate:** Coordinate your cocktail, wine, and menu selections. Keep it simple and use fresh ingredients whenever possible. Don't experiment at your party; stick with reliable recipes. Very important—prepare as much as you can ahead of time.
* **Vision:** Seeing is feeling. Serve your guests a beautiful signature cocktail as they arrive. This not only relaxes your guests, but gives them a visual signal of things to come. Lighting greatly affects the vibe of your party, so plan accordingly. While candlelight is always best for night, most times it does not cast enough light for dining. Invest in a dimmer(s) for your dining/living room(s)/entertaining space; it will help to create the perfect mood while maintaining the ambiance of your candlelight.
* **Aroma:** Allow a "good" food aroma to waft through the air. Scent memory is powerful and can instantly create a warm feeling associated with a fond memory of a place or time (e.g., the smell of cotton candy can bring us back to memories of being a child at a summer fair). Make sure to buy unscented candles to avoid overpowering the senses. The exception to this rule is in the powder room.
* **Acoustics:** Music is instrumental. Prepare your music mix in advance and coordinate it with the vibe of your party. Music has the incredible power to relax, excite, inspire, and transport people to another place mentally.
* **Feel:** Connect with your guests. What guest would not feel special knowing their host specially prepared this party just for them? Make time for conversation and show your guests that you are happy they are in your home sharing time with you.

....

BUILDER'S NOTE: Begin and end on a personal note. Make your guests feel extra special by sending a personalized invitation and end with a keepsake from the evening. Gestures like these make a further personal connection between you and your guests.

Why Entertain in Your Home?

PARTY WITH A PURPOSE

*I am thankful for the mess to clean after a party
because it means I have been surrounded by friends.*
—Nancie J. Carmody

1 **It is an opportunity** to nurture relationships. When you invite guests into your home, you are inviting them into your personal space and offering them an invitation to connect with you and vice versa.

2 **It is a way for you** to socialize with family and friends whenever you want to. Today, family and friends live further apart, schedules are jam-packed, and it's not as easy to spend time together. With some forethought, planning and preparation, you can create these opportunities to socialize. Whether you pick up the phone and invite friends over for a drink spur of the moment, invite guests over after an event, just want to spend time with friends and family, or have an occasion to celebrate, you can make it happen.

3 **It is an economical alternative** to hosting a party in a public venue. Control costs by setting a time, style, and menu that fits your budget.

4 **It is good for you** (and your guests). It is a proven fact that people who socialize more are healthier mentally, emotionally, and physically than those who do not. Medical research has proven time and time again that laughter is good medicine. What do people usually end up doing at parties? Laughing and having fun.

5 **It is a liberating experience** to have a successful party in your home. You have complete control and creative license over all aspects of your party. It also builds your self-confidence as you realize that you can be a great host.

6 **It is fulfilling and satisfying** to experience partying with a purpose (nurturing relationships and forging new ones). What a fun way to enrich your lifestyle!

OUR APPROACH TO ENTERTAINING provides you with strategies, techniques, tools, and plans to enrich your lifestyle. But, the "U" in Partybluprints is "YOU." As you build your party, remember you are the key element:

> You can infuse your personality into your party—share something new with your guests. Your personal touches will make you and your guests feel special.
> You can set a positive and fun tone for the party—your guests will follow your lead.
> You can be a guest at your party—feel the vibe, enjoy the cocktails, food, music, and your guests.
> You have the power to create an experience for you and your guests in your home.
> You have the ability to bring more joy, love, and fun into your home by sharing it with others.

You Are the Key Element

HERE ARE SOME ACTION STEPS you can follow as you commit to a new approach to entertaining—Plan to Party.

These steps involve reflection, analysis, planning and preparing; however, this investment of time up front will have a big payoff. You'll not only be prepared to entertain in your home, you'll be more excited to do it—hence, less stress, more fun and confidence!

❖ **Be organized.** A well-developed plan can make your party. We realize just how important a foundation is and that is why we are providing you with four Party Plans to get you started. Use them as your set of "bluprints" for building your party and also as reference in creating your own party plans.

❖ **Be realistic.** A written plan forces you to give your party some thought and find the balance between your expectations and what is realistic. Once "planned," you know the steps you need to follow to reach your goal—a fabulous party.

❖ **Be smart.** Take into account your available resources when deciding how to invest your time or money in a well thought out and developed plan.

❖ **Be productive.** Working smart and working hard are two different things. Think through what you need to accomplish, get organized, and then get it done.

❖ **Be prepared.** Prepare yourself, your home, your tools, and your party. Give yourself enough time to prepare in advance and use tools such as a Materials List (shopping list) and Critical Path (timeline/to-do list) (see examples at the end of each plan) with the intent to have everything prepared before your first guest walks through the door.

❖ **Be thorough.** Having a plan is not enough—you must follow your plan to build your party. You will reap the rewards of creating a plan and sticking to it. All your hard work will result in a special time shared by you and your guests.

❖ **Be committed.** Remove any and all potential barriers to reaching your entertaining goals.

How to Plan

REMOVE COMMON BARRIERS
TO ENTERTAINING

LACK OF SELF-CONFIDENCE | Whether hosting a cocktail party or a sit-down dinner in your home, it is important to feel comfortable and confident. Believe in yourself. If you do not, nobody else will. Share the best "you" with your guests. Banish negative thoughts: "I can't do this," "It's not perfect," "I can't entertain as well as my friends," etc. Instead, encourage and motivate yourself with an "I can do it and I will do it" positive attitude. If confidence is a real problem for you, then start out small. Have a couple of friends over for cocktails or have a small dinner party with just one other couple and build your confidence.

FEAR OF THE FIRST PARTY | Everyone has a first party, then a second, and a third—the next thing you know, you are a proficient host. All of your friends will be asking for your advice, and you will be able to give it. Host your first party.

TIME | If you stress about finding the time to plan and prepare for a party, be "time-wise." Do not leave shopping, cleaning your house, and preparing your food for the day of the party. Whatever you can prepare ahead of time, do so. The recipes included in our Party Plans can be prepared before the party, and we include a Critical Path (timeline/to-do list) in each plan to help you complete your tasks. Our timelines will help you balance your everyday responsibilities with your "party tasks" so you can easily stay on track and be efficient while executing your plan for your party. Plus, we have done all the legwork in designing and developing the party plan, so before you even lift a finger, you have saved a significant amount of time.

MONEY | Bigger is not always better. Whatever your budget is, use it wisely, and host your party from the heart. You can host unique parties with less money than you think. You just have to be creative with your resources. A well-developed plan is a smart place to start. Find a style that works for entertaining in your home, own it, and treat your guests to an intimate and unique experience created by you just for them.

THINKING YOUR GUESTS WILL NOT ENJOY YOUR PARTY | If you are worried guests will not enjoy your party, believe us, they will! You are creating an experience (a gift) just for them—who wouldn't feel special?

NOT KNOWING WHAT KIND OF PARTY TO HOST | Review our Party Plans in Section Three and select one that fits your needs or use them for inspiration.

STRESS | Having a well-developed plan eliminates the unknown factors that produce stress while planning and preparing for a party. Follow your plan and timeline and do not panic—you have everything under control.

THINKING YOUR HOUSE IS NOT CLEAN OR GOOD ENOUGH | In many families and cultures, an invitation to someone's home is considered a great honor. A home is sacred and private. The honor is conveyed in the unwritten part of the invitation, "I consider you special and I want to share my home with you." So get your home in order (see "Define and Prepare the 'Footprint' of your Entertaining Space") and remind yourself, an invitation to your home is an honor.

BUILD YOUR FOUNDATION

ONCE YOU HAVE REMOVED any barriers to entertaining, it is time to focus on building and fortifying your foundation. Here are a few steps to get you started:

1. DEFINE AND PREPARE THE "FOOTPRINT" OF YOUR ENTERTAINING SPACE

> Select one room in your home to be your "entertaining space."

> After defining your entertaining space, clean it. Remove all clutter and extraneous "stuff" from all table and counter surfaces to provide room to place drinks and plates. Display coasters for drinks on tables to avoid damage from water rings from glasses.

> Arrange furniture to be conducive for chatting and mingling. Vignettes work well—a vignette is a "scene or setting." Use this idea to create a few cozy seating areas that include small group seating and a surface to rest a drink and plate.

> Lighting is key to setting the right mood for any party. Make sure you can adjust your lighting to fit your vibe and have an ample supply of candles.

> Make your room music-ready. If you do not have a music system in your home, consider an iPod and docking station.

> Prepare a spot for coats, jackets, and purses. If your closet is not capable of housing these items, arrange for an alternative location or consider a collapsible movable garment rack that you can place out of sight.

> In addition to your "entertaining space," you will need to make sure your powder room is prepped for guests. Keep an extra set of hand towels, a special liquid soap and a scented candle on hand. Just before guests arrive replace your towels and soap with a fresh supply and light the candle. Disinfecting wipes, glass cleaner and paper towels do wonders in five minutes, so keep them handy. Finally, change out the toilet paper roll for a full roll (and leave an extra roll). Also, make sure there is a full box of tissues available.

2. INVENTORY YOUR TOOLS

A crucial step in entertaining is being "equipped" to entertain. It is a fact that any job is easier if you have the proper tools and know how to use them. Tools allow you to be more efficient in completing the job and producing a better result.

Based on years of practical experience, we have compiled a checklist of basic materials, the Partybluprints Essentials Checklist. We consider it our "toolbox"; use it as a guide. You'll find the Partybluprints Essentials Checklist at the end of this section, pgs. 56–59.

3. FOLLOW A PARTYBLUPRINTS PARTY PLAN | See Section Three—Party Plans.

4. DRAFT YOUR OWN SET OF BLUPRINTS/PARTY PLAN | We'll approach this in two stages: (1) Preliminary Planning, and (2) Developing Your Specs (Party Components).

BUILDER'S NOTE: Once you have completed Foundation Exercise #1 (above) with one room, expand your "footprint" to include a few other areas.

PRELIMINARY PLANNING

When planning a party or gathering, there are a few areas you must address in advance of detailing the specifications (specs) for your party plan. This will help define your scope (concept) and core elements (foundation).

> **Budget** | What is your budget? If you do not know, sit down and set one. Then follow it.

> **Timeline** | How many weeks/days do you have until the party? Be realistic. Leave yourself an appropriate amount of time to plan, execute, and prepare when you set the party date. Do not try to squeeze a month's work of planning and preparation into a week. Remember a happy host results in happy guests.

> **Time and Resource Bank** | How much time and effort are you able or willing to invest in this party? There is nothing worse than planning a party and being frazzled, stressed-out, and exhausted when the party date finally arrives because you underestimated your available resources.

Use the Five "W's" to Determine the Parameters of Your Plan:
Who, What, Where, When and Why:

WHO	Adults, children, families, women only, or guys only
	Determine how many people will be there:
	1. Intimate: 2–8 guests
	2. Medium: 8–20 guests
	3. Large: More than 20 guests
WHAT	Brunch, luncheon, dinner, dessert, cocktails
WHERE	Indoors or outdoors, dining room, family room, etc.
WHEN	Late morning, early afternoon, mid-day, evening, late-night
WHY	Birthday, anniversary, wedding, milestone event, or just to get together

IMPORTANT: Once you have a handle on who your guests are and whether it is a crowd or intimate group, determine your vibe (what type of atmosphere you want to achieve with your party—formal, informal, festive, laid-back, "mingling mixer," etc.)

BUILDER'S NOTE: Reference the Party Plans in Section Three, specifically the Critical Path (timeline/to-do list), to get a good idea of tasks and timelines involved.

Defining Your Entertaining Style

A FEW POINTS TO CONSIDER

Embrace your lifestyle, your skill set, and your available time, resources, and budget. Incorporate your love for spending time with friends and family in your home, and determine the type of entertaining that is right for you during this particular time in your life.

For example, if you have babies and young children, you may not be able to host formal dinner parties. Family barbeques or brunches may be better suited for your present lifestyle. This does not mean you will never host a formal dinner party. Do what you can while working towards what you aspire to do.

Develop an entertaining style that is simple and special, and expand upon that foundation as your circumstances change. Do not avoid entertaining because this phase of your life is not conducive to it. Your entertaining style will evolve throughout your life. Start where you are today. Adapt your entertaining to fit your lifestyle. The important thing is to do it—no more excuses, just get started. Make time to plan.

Time, Money, and Stress Management

A FEW OF OUR FAVORITE SHORTCUTS

IF YOUR BUDGET ALLOWS, you may decide to pay for some "conveniences." If your time is more valuable than doing a task yourself, or you simply don't have the time, see if you can incorporate any of these time-saving services into your budget. Otherwise, employ some strategies to save time and effort while doing it all yourself.

❖ Order materials online and have them delivered right to your front doorstep. Make sure to order well in advance to avoid paying excessive shipping charges.

❖ Order a fabulous dessert if you are not a good baker or just don't have the time to bake.

❖ Rent glasses from a company that delivers clean stemware and picks up dirty ones. Then, there are no dirty glasses to wash post-party; simply put them back in the crate they came in for pickup the next day.

❖ Hire someone to clean your home, particularly your first floor and your party area. If you have other bathrooms in your home, close the door of your powder room and do not let anyone use it until the party. Get some help rearranging furniture or bringing in furniture such as tables, chairs, buffet, or bar, etc.

❖ Hire a bartender or server.

❖ Have tablecloths ironed and placed on tables. Now the stage is set and you are free to work your magic.

❖ Set your tables, bars, and buffets the night before your party with all non-perishable items.

❖ Determine how much you are willing to spend on invitations, cocktails, food, music, special activities, favors, and tablescape items. If you have extra money in your budget, fresh flowers always enhance any space.

❖ Start the process early, and leave yourself plenty of time to plan and execute your plan. Make a decision as to whether you are willing to spend money to save time and effort (see some options above) or whether you will do it all yourself. If you are trying to keep costs down, your "sweat equity" is much cheaper than paying someone else to do it. However, if you do not leave yourself enough time, you may find yourself in a position where you feel you do not have a choice but to hire someone to cook and clean. You may also find yourself making impulse purchases and overbuying because you are panicking and not sticking to your plan. Never, ever panic.

ARCHITECT'S NOTE: Our mantra is "simple and special." A tight budget does not mean you cannot create an experience for your guests. A well thought out and coordinated plan that addresses all the senses yields a tremendous return on your upfront investment.

BRUNCH BASICS

AS A HOST, brunches can be an extremely fun, economical, and enjoyable way to entertain if you follow our Brunch Basics Guide. **Here are some practical and easy tips for hosting a successful stress-free brunch:**

❖ **Serve the right balance of breakfast and lunch foods.**

Why? Guests will fall into 1 of 3 categories:

> **Breakfast Food Fan** | Strictly interested in breakfast and is not putting a lunch item on the plate.

> **Ready for Lunch Lover** | Breakfast is so over by eleven, let's have lunch.

> **True brunch aficionado** | Two types:

  1. **Brunch Lover** | Deftly crafts a plate combining breakfast and lunch items enjoying both in one sitting;

  2. **Brunch Marathoner** | Keeps a steady pace through courses starting with breakfast and working right through lunch.

❖ **Choose foods that are delicious and safe to eat after sitting out at room temperature for one and a half hours, or hot dishes that hold up on a hot plate or in a chafing dish for the same amount of time.**

Why? Your guests are guaranteed to arrive sporadically anytime from your invite time until thirty minutes later. Also, this gives your guests the freedom to enjoy the buffet at their leisure.

❖ **Select dishes that can be prepared ahead of time and displayed before your first guest arrives.**

Why? So you can be a guest at your own party!

SOME MENU SUGGESTIONS:

Breakfast Foods | Frittata, French toast casserole, crepes with fresh fruit and crème, croissants—a twist on brunch standards: eggs, pancakes, and French toast.

BUILDER'S NOTE: If children are among your guests, serve kid favorites such as: French toast sticks, sausage and bacon.

Lunch Foods | Spiral Ham and Make Your Own Salad Bar—our favorite brunch items for versatility, ease of preparation, and serving (great for feeding a crowd).

❖ **Spiral Ham** | Remove from wrapper, heat, glaze, and serve (it can be served warm to room temperature).

> If you love breakfast, enjoy it as your breakfast meat side. Conversely, if you are a lunch fan, make a gourmet ham sandwich on a croissant.

> It is the perfect leftover when all the guests are gone!

❖ **Make Your Own Salad Bar** | Alongside a big bowl of lightly dressed spring greens, offer any selection of toppings beautifully presented on platters that guests can enjoy on their salad or as sides. Our suggestions:

> **Cheese plate** | Serve Parmigiano Reggiano in a wedge that guests can grate on their salad, frittata, or sandwich; others may take a nugget to savor on the side of their meal.

> **Fruit platter** | Turn a basic salad into a citrus or berry salad or mix it up for a breakfast side or healthy dessert.
> **Nuts** (almonds, walnuts) | Display in a pedestal dish as some snacking morsels or as a protein boost with the greens.
> **Roasted vegetables** | They are a decadent addition to greens, and you can also make a meal of them (perfect for the non-meat eaters) or as a delicious side to any breakfast, lunch, or brunch plate.

BASIC BRUNCH TIPS:

> Set up dishes, napkins, and flatware on surface near buffet. If you have enough room to seat all your guests, preset your table with place cards and allow each guest to find their spot, fill their glass and then take their plate to the buffet. This prevents a balancing act with beverage and utensils. If you do not have enough space to seat your guests at tables, make sure you bring in extra seating and offer flat surfaces for drinks near the seating.
> Depending upon the number of guests, collect a variety of dinner dishes from your kitchen and borrow the rest. Do the same with flatware. Having a variety is very vintage. This saves you money on paper products and generates less waste.

> Set up a "help yourself" beverage station with a signature cocktail (our favorites: French 75, sparkling wine, Prosecco, Champagne), pitchers/carafes of fruit-infused water, sparkling water, and iced tea. You may choose to offer wine and beer, but do not get into offering too many selections. If you do, before you know it, you will be setting up a full bar. Keep it simple!
> **Buffet** | Set up your buffet. Identify which serving dishes and utensils you will need for each menu item and arrange them on the buffet surface. This can be a time sucker if left until the day of the brunch. Use extra place cards to identify each dish. If space allows, place an eye-catching floral arrangement in the center of your buffet. If you simply do not have the space, create small satellite arrangements, and place them throughout the area where your guests will be dining and mingling. Resist the temptation to add sparkle to your buffet with candlesticks—they're never a good idea when guests are reaching and may be distracted by chit-chat in the buffet line.
> Set up a separate Dessert Buffet with endless luscious and decadent desserts. Everyone will remember this! Include coffee, tea, cream, sugar, cups, spoons, dessert plates, and napkins.

HIGH IMPACT LOOKS FOR LESS

FEELING THE PINCH ON YOUR PARTY because of a tight budget, but still want a big impact? You can create high party impact on a low party budget with a technique we call "mass appeal." The key to creating a rich look with inexpensive items is to group a multitude of them in the same color (or color family). A monochromatic mass can take a rather mundane item and make it look WOW (glamorous, dramatic, or just fun). Here are a few examples of how we have utilized this concept in several of our Party Plans:

1 **Carnations**: Group these inexpensive flowers en masse and transform ordinary into dramatic. (See how we used them in our Chocolate Soiree Party Plan, pg. 211–212.)

2 **Votive Candles/Floating Candles**: For evening soirees, use votive candles and/or floating candles en masse to set your party aglow—very glamorous. (See how we used the votives in our Chocolate Soiree Party Plan, pg. 211, and floating candles in our A Night in Venice Party Plan, pg. 169.)

3 **Dessert Bars/"Sweet Bars"**: These are a dynamite idea for dessert and can double as the take-home favor, too. Serve up candies, cookies, brownies and/or cake in one color to delight and amuse your guests. The use of a monochromatic colorscape transforms less expensive and glamorous desserts into a fun and festive array of goodies without looking like you're pinching pennies (plus, you'll find guests love food that makes them feel like a kid again). (See how we used it in our What a Girl Wants Party Plan, pg. 260.)

VIBE

It's not about the food, it's about the mood. —*Arnie Mascali*

❖ **Remember our Essence of Entertaining** when coordinating all your party elements, and don't forget about the vibe. Deciding on a vibe is a great way to make sure all your elements are in sync and serve to enhance the vibe, and not detract from it.

❖ **Use the five Ws** (who, what, where, when and why) to help determine your vibe. For example, the vibe at a late morning family-style brunch is going to be much different than an adult-only cocktail party. Use coordinated elements such as music, food, beverages, flowers, tablescape elements, color, and various types of lighting to create your vibe. To get comfortable with the concept, take a look at our four different Party Plans—the vibe is noted on the first page of each. Then, look through the specs and footprint to see how we created a vibe using the elements in each section.

DEVELOPING YOUR SPECS:
PARTY COMPONENTS

NOW THAT YOU have completed your preliminary planning, it is time to develop your specs (party elements): Invitations, Cocktails, Food, Music, Special Activities and Favors.

INVITATIONS

Who does not love to receive an invitation? Make sure to deliver yours in a special and unique way. Whether it's by mail, phone, or email, devote some time and effort to the message and spirit you want to send your guests. Excite them with your invitation. Your invitation sets the tone for the party way before the first guest arrives, so start on a personal note.

COCKTAILS

Take pride in your cocktails and give the "cocktail" portion of your party or a cocktail party some forethought and attention. Develop a strategy for an easy way to serve cocktails at your next party (you will use this at every party you host!).

FOOD

Start simple and stay simple. If you're inclined to try a new recipe on company, do not. Select a menu you can prepare ahead of time. If you are looking to introduce a special element into your menu, use fresh ingredients. This "simple and special" twist is easy, economical, and creates a big impact.

MUSIC

Music is a must at any party. Create a music mix in advance that matches the vibe of your party.

SPECIAL ACTIVITIES

Introduce an activity at your party, such as wine tasting and chocolate tasting. Engaging in a shared experience offers guests an opportunity to connect with each other.

FAVORS

End your party with a keepsake from the evening. It is a great opportunity to send your guests off with a special "good night" treat and/or message.

BUILDER'S NOTE: Finally, don't forget about your detailed specs (these are the flow of your party and tablescape). Design a tablescape (the landscape of your table/party) that represents your vibe. Depending upon the type of party, you can carry the elements of your tablescape throughout your home, including dining table, buffet table, and other stations. This is why it's important to design a flow for your party, to determine how your guests are going to move from one area (cocktails) to the next (food) and in between. See the Detailed Specs in our Party Plans for more information and inspiration.

COCKTAIL HOUR PRIMER

IF YOU THINK being a "good" host means offering a full bar, think again. The effort and expense required to set one up can be substantial. In addition, you need ample space to display the liquor, mixers, and barware required for a full bar. Further, at the end of the night, you are left with a big mess to clean up.

GO SIMPLE AND SPECIAL. With some advance planning and attention to detail, less can definitely be much more. Offer a specially designed cocktail as well as a few additional alcoholic beverages and non-alcoholic alternatives.

HERE'S HOW:

SELECT A SIGNATURE COCKTAIL FOR YOUR PARTY. Choose a cocktail that "fits" your party. This approach involves some work prior to your party, taste testing cocktail recipes!

FACTORS TO CONSIDER:

> **Season** | Summer vs. holiday, hot vs. cold.

> **Theme** | Make sure your cocktail complements your party (vibe, menu, etc.). You can make your "cocktail" your theme, e.g., artisan beer tasting, wine tasting, martini party, scotch tasting.

> **Keep it simple** | Unless you are hiring a bartender to mix drinks all night and keep the line moving, serve a cocktail that you can pour in one shot (sparkling wine, martinis, any cocktail that keeps well when made in advance and stored

in a pitcher or original bottle).

> **Taste test** | To narrow your selection, taste test a few recipes. Once you decide on your cocktail, make sure you are comfortable with your recipe (tweak it to suit your taste) and practice preparing it. This is the best research and development (R&D) you will ever do!

IN ADDITION TO YOUR SIGNATURE COCKTAIL, OFFER THE FOLLOWING:

> **Wine** | A red and white choice.

> **Beer** | Regular and light varieties.

> **Alternative beverages** | Sparkling water, regular water, and soda are good staples.

> **Mocktails** | If you know any of your guests don't or can't drink, offer a special non-alcoholic cocktail.

HOW TO SERVE:

We also recommend having two dozen wine glasses on hand. Wash and dry them (make sure they are spot free) and then line them up for self-service in your designated "bar area." Have a few bottles

---

BUILDER'S NOTE: Gather a collection of glasses. While some glasses need to fit the drink (sparkling wine/flutes, martinis/martini glasses), most other cocktails can be served in rocks glasses and/or stemless wine glasses.

*Cocktail party: A gathering held to enable forty people
to talk about themselves at the same time.
The man who remains after the liquor is gone is the host.*
—Fred Allen

of wine uncorked so when guests are finished with their "cocktail," they can help themselves to a glass of wine or a beer (in our experience, most people prefer drinking beer straight from the bottle and it avoids additional glassware; however, have some glasses on hand for those who like their beer in a glass). You can also offer your alternative beverages in this same location. Provide double the amount of wine glasses and use for alternative beverages.

This approach to cocktail hour or a cocktail party also avoids a designated bartender (no one wants to play bartender all night, unless they're getting paid for it). So serve your guests their first drink and then let them help themselves.

DON'T FORGET:

> **Appetizers/snacks**
Always have food available when serving cocktails. Depending on whether you're hosting a casual or more formal cocktail party, select appetizers to suit your gathering. For ideas and inspirations, visit us at The Partybluprints Blog, www.partybluprintsblog.com.

After your last guest has departed, the cleanup is simple. Rinse all the wine and beer bottles and toss them in the recycling bin. Fill your "glasses crate" (see our Entertaining Essentials Checklist) with the dirty glasses. Cover it with a dish towel, store it out of the way and deal with it in the morning.

BUILDER'S NOTE: There are many good value wines, so do your homework or find a local wine expert whose recommendations you trust. You'll find him/her to be an invaluable resource. For more information on wine and wine tasting, see our Wine Country Crush Party Plan, pgs. 64–119.

FRESH AND NATURAL FOODS

IF YOU ARE LUCKY ENOUGH to have your own garden or live near a farmer's market or grocery store with a fabulous produce section, buy whatever is in season and sauté, grill, roast, or enjoy it raw. Fresh produce makes everyone feel good. Seek out a local farmer's market in your area; it's great way to support your local farmers.

Some of our favorite (and simple) ways to use fresh ingredients to transform ordinary into extraordinary include:

❖ **Fresh limes and lemons** | Their juice immediately makes any cocktail or dish bright and delicious. If you don't have access to good fresh produce throughout the seasons, fresh citrus (lemons, limes and oranges) is a great way to incorporate a flavor that's invigorating. Some examples: Our favorite French 75 is delicious with fresh lemon juice (see our version at www.partybluprintsblog.com, search "DIY French 75 Cocktail") or prepare fresh salsa or hummus with fresh lime or lemon juice.

❖ **Fresh berries** | Raspberries, strawberries, blackberries and blueberries—their color and taste make you smile. They always feel like a decadent treat whether you serve them as a garnish in a cocktail, as a surprise in a green salad, or simply mixed as a dessert. As a bonus, berries are full of healthy antioxidants.

❖ **Fresh herbs and vegetables** | Basil, parsley, mint, cilantro, rosemary—there is no denying the difference fresh herbs make. They have the power to transform any ordinary dish, pasta, meat, chicken, vegetables, grains, or whatever you are preparing into something extraordinary. The same goes for fresh vegetables (baked, grilled, roasted or raw). Herbs are one of the easiest ways to cook "simple and special." Grow your own herbs or purchase from your local supermarket. A little goes a long way.

❖ **Infused water** | Infuse a pitcher or carafe of water with a fruit, vegetable or herb that complements your appetizers, meal or dessert. Try berries, citrus, cucumbers, or mint—experiment by infusing a single glass of water to determine your preference.

Builder's Note: A few hours before serving, simply fill container with water, add selected produce that has been thoroughly cleaned and cut if necessary (e.g., citrus, cucumbers), cover and set aside for an hour or two. The water will slowly become infused with the essence of the produce. One to two hours before serving, chill infused water.

❖ **Infused cocktails:** For a fresh taste, use your own infused spirits in lieu of purchasing infused spirits. Become a "liquovore" and bring the locavore sensation into the world of cocktail mixing. Bring your beverage home by mixing locally grown herbs, vegetables, or fruit with a clean spirit.

In addition to eating and accenting, fresh produce makes for fabulous centerpieces. For high impact, choose monochromatic produce—remember our "mass appeal" technique.

PARTYBLUPRINTS RULE OF GOOD MEASURE

"When you can, always use fresh ingredients."

1. It makes every recipe taste more special.

2. It's simple to incorporate fresh ingredients.

3. In most cases it's a healthier option.

OUTDOOR ENTERTAINING

THE ABCS OF OUTDOOR ENTERTAINING

KEEP YOUR GUESTS COMFORTABLE

A. **Banish the bugs.** One hour before guests arrive, light citronella candles or spray bug repellent around perimeter of party. Have individual bug spray wipes and/or spray on hand for guests' convenience and to be used at their discretion.

B. **Offer your guests the opportunity to "wash" with wipes and/or hand sanitizer.** A must have at a picnic!

C. **Give your guests a place to kick back.** Provide plenty of clean and comfortable seating (chairs, blankets, benches, etc.). For the kids, arrange one or two blankets for them on the ground or deck. If they have a spill, you can simply fold the blankets up and wash them later. Have an extra blanket for the kids to play and relax on after eating.

KEEP WASTE TO A MINIMUM

A. **Mark your beverages.** For disposable cups and bottles, use stickers that adhere to container. Using a permanent pen, have each guest mark their sticker with their name or initials. For glasses, use a removable adhesive or glass marker/tag. This avoids waste as guests inevitably forget where they set their drink—all they have to do is remember the symbol/sticker on their cup.

B. **Put out a recycling bin** for empties and point it out to your guests.

C. **Use renewable dinnerware** or acrylic dishware and cloth napkins. For fun, you can purchase flag bandanas and use them as napkins.

KEEP IT COOL AND WET

A. **Ice, ice, and more ice.** There is nothing worse than lukewarm beverages on a hot day. Make sure you have more than enough ice to continually replenish the supply. A general rule of thumb is two pounds of ice per person.

B. **Hydrate your guests.** Have plenty of non-alcoholic beverages on hand. Make sure to consider all your guests: adults, children, and the elderly.

C. **Offer shade.** Create some with a few umbrellas. You can also purchase a fan (or two) that mists while it cools—now that's cool!

KEEP IT HEALTHY

A. **Use vinaigrette,** not mayonnaise, to dress salads. Mayonnaise can spoil quickly when temperatures are soaring.

B. **Do not set up your buffet table** in direct sunlight; use either natural shade or an umbrella as a buffer. Do not leave food out on buffet table longer than one hour.

C. **For those sun lovers** who forgot to put lotion on at home, put out some spray suntan lotion for easy and convenient protection from the sun.

For more ideas and inspirations on Outdoor Entertaining, visit us at www.partybluprintsblog.com.

GREEN ENTERTAINING

FIVE TIPS FOR KEEPING THE PLANET ALIVE WHEN YOU PARTY!

1 **Reduce your carbon footprint** by taking a virtual trip. Turn your home into your chosen destination. Invoke the spirit of that region in the comfort of your own home. (See how we did it with our Wine Country Crush and A Night in Venice Party Plans.)

2 **Grow your own herb garden.** Plant herbs such as basil, mint, parsley, thyme, rosemary, and cilantro and you will be ready, at a moment's notice, to spice up any cocktail, dish, or dessert—no driving necessary. Fresh herbs have the power to transform simple meat, fish, pasta, and produce (whatever you have on hand) into a fabulously fresh dish.

3 **Use fresh produce** or flowering plants as your centerpiece(s). A day or two after your party, use the fresh produce for cooking purposes. You can place the flowering plants in your garden or send them home with your guests to plant in their garden as a remembrance of your gathering.

4 **Use your dishes** instead of buying paper plates from the local party store or supermarket.

For indoor entertaining, use your china (that is why you have it, right?) or everyday dishes.

For outdoor entertaining, purchase melamine plates that you can reuse party after party. You will recoup your initial investment after a few uses.

If you are worried about cleanup, do not be. Scrape the plates, stack them, and worry about them later if you can't fit them in your dishwasher.

5 **Use electronic invitations.** This saves paper and all the energy that is involved in getting mail from one place to the next. Remember to include your personal touch on electronic invitations.

PARTYBLUPRINTS ESSENTIALS CHECKLIST—OUR TOOLBOX

PARTYBLUPRINTS PICKS | Everyday Kitchen Essentials

Once you have these tools, you will not need to replace them until they wear out or break:

ELECTRIC SMALL APPLIANCES

- ☐ Heavy-duty blender
- ☐ Microwave
- ☐ Coffee pot
- ☐ Hand-held mixer
- ☐ Mini food processor

POTS AND PANS

- ☐ Stockpot (8 qt.) heavy gauge aluminum nonstick with lid
- ☐ Stockpot (10 or 12 qt.) heavy gauge aluminum nonstick with lid
- ☐ Sauce pan with lid (4.5 qt.) heavy gauge aluminum nonstick with lid
- ☐ Skillet (12-in.) heavy gauge aluminum nonstick with lid
- ☐ Griddle (10 x 18-in.) hard anodized nonstick
- ☐ 13 x 9-in. baking sheets (2)
- ☐ Pizza pan
- ☐ Roasting pan (16 x 13-in.)
- ☐ Wire cooling racks (2)

BAKING DISHES

- ☐ Pyrex glass pie dish (9-in.)
- ☐ Pyrex glass baking dish (13 x 9-in.)

BOWLS

- ☐ Melamine nested bowls (choose a color you love)
- ☐ Pyrex glass bowl (2.5 L)
- ☐ Large shallow bowl for salad or pasta
- ☐ Covered casserole dishes (large and small)

DISHWARE FOR 12

- ☐ Dinner plates
- ☐ Soup/salad bowls
- ☐ Luncheon/dessert plates

GLASSWARE FOR 12

- ☐ Coffee mugs/cups
- ☐ Wine glasses:
  - ☐ Red wine glasses
  - ☐ White wine glasses
  - ☐ Stemless wine glasses (you can also use these for serving water, cocktails, or non-alcoholic beverages)
- ☐ Champagne flutes
- ☐ Water glasses

FLATWARE

- ☐ Place settings (12)
- ☐ Serving pieces

ARCHITECT'S NOTE: We recommend a set of white dishes; they are versatile, and it's easy to accessorize them any way you wish depending on the event or season—consider them your "little black dress" for entertaining.

PARTYBLUPRINTS ESSENTIALS CHECKLIST—OUR TOOLBOX

LINENS

- [ ] White tablecloth (sized to fit your dining table)
- [ ] Cloth napkins (12)
- [ ] Dish towels
- [ ] Apron

MISC.

- [ ] Gas lighter with extender handle

SERVING DISHES (PLAIN WHITE)

- [ ] Large oval platter
- [ ] Rectangular/square platter
- [ ] Cheese plate/board (can be ceramic, wooden, slate)

KITCHEN TOOLS

- [ ] Pyrex glass liquid measuring cups (1 and 2 cup)
- [ ] Colander
- [ ] Cutting boards (3)
- [ ] Heat resistant spatulas (2)
- [ ] Plastic spatulas (2)
- [ ] Dry measuring cups
- [ ] Nested measuring spoons
- [ ] Wooden spoons (2)
- [ ] Ladle
- [ ] Cheese grater
- [ ] Tongs
- [ ] Meat thermometer

- [ ] 3 knives (chef's, serrated, paring)
- [ ] Vegetable peeler
- [ ] Toothpicks

CONDIMENT SERVERS

- [ ] Sugar and creamer
- [ ] Pepper mill
- [ ] Salt mill
- [ ] Butter dish
- [ ] Salad dressing cruet

STAPLES

- [ ] Plastic wrap
- [ ] Tin foil
- [ ] Plastic bags
- [ ] Kitchen garbage bags
- [ ] Paper towels
- [ ] Toilet paper
- [ ] Spices (pepper, salt, garlic powder, basil, oregano, parsley, chili powder, etc.)—they are at their freshest up to 6 months after opening
- [ ] Spices for baking (cinnamon, baking powder, baking soda, cream of tartar)
- [ ] Olive oil (one for cooking can be average quality)
- [ ] Olive oil (best you can afford for dipping/dressings)
- [ ] Balsamic vinegar/red wine vinegar
- [ ] Sea salt

ARCHITECT'S NOTE: If you are entertaining more than 12 guests, including you, you will need an additional supply of items noted as "for 12" in Everyday Kitchen Essentials

PARTYBLUPRINTS ESSENTIALS CHECKLIST—OUR TOOLBOX

PARTYBLUPRINTS PICKS | Entertaining Essentials

In addition to your Everyday Kitchen Essentials, these items are essential when you have a crowd. After each party, clean them, replenish as necessary, and store until the next party.

GENERAL

- ☐ Collapsible tables—depends on your available space/existing tables/size and type of entertaining you like to do
- ☐ Folding chairs—depends on existing seating/size and type of entertaining you like to do
- ☐ White tablecloth (cleaned and pressed, sized to fit collapsible table)
- ☐ Plastic restaurant glass crate (bin with dividers for storing glassware); regardless of whether you entertain four or twenty people, there will be plenty of dirty glasses—this is a great place to store them and put them away for later
- ☐ In addition to a set of everyday white plates, you may opt to keep a set or two of clear glass dinner plates and dessert plates for entertaining a crowd

COCKTAIL PARTY/COCKTAIL HOUR

Keep your essential cocktail party/cocktail hour necessities in an easily accessible spot so you will have what you need at a moment's notice.

- ☐ Cocktail shaker
- ☐ Shot glasses (1 oz. and 2 oz.)
- ☐ Rocks glasses

- ☐ Martini glasses—multi-purpose, serve appetizers and dessert in them, too
- ☐ Agave syrup—time-saving substitute for simple syrup
- ☐ Cocktail napkins
- ☐ Square white cocktail plates
- ☐ Appetizer forks
- ☐ Cheese board—large wooden board and smaller square board/slate
- ☐ Cheese utensils—a variety of cheese knives for various texture cheeses
- ☐ Interestingly shaped white appetizer serving platters—long skinny rectangular, square compartmentalized, oval, and/or round
- ☐ Votives and tea lights (2 dozen)
- ☐ Pillar candles (2)
- ☐ Ice bucket

WINE ESSENTIALS

- ☐ Wine glasses
- ☐ Corkscrew
- ☐ Cheesecloth—use to salvage wine from a broken cork
- ☐ Wine decanter (optional)

NOTES

$\cdots\cdots\cdots$

BUILDER'S NOTE: Create your own Emergency Entertaining Kit. We suggest you compile your own kit based on the type of entertaining you like to do on short notice. Stock your key items and you will always be ready to informally entertain guests at the blink of an eye. Here are some suggestions to get you started: non-perishable snacks (nuts, breadsticks, chocolate, crackers, etc.), a few perishable snacks (wedge of parmesan cheese, pepperoni, roasted red peppers, olives, etc.), non-alcoholic beverages (seltzer, soda, juice, etc.), alcoholic beverages (whatever you and your guests like to drink—wine, martinis, beer, etc.). Remember, create a kit to suit your needs.

We have covered quite a bit
of basic material in this section.
Now it's time to move
into the actual Party Plans.
Familiarize yourself with our
Party Plans, and be inspired.
Try one or two or all and then
have fun developing your own.

Party Plans

THINK OF OUR PARTY PLANS like a set of bluprints. We start each plan at the foundation, providing a broad overview of the party. Then, we get right into the specifics, laying out every detail you will need. Like an architect, we planned for everything you need to build your party, from space, to menu, to the intangible vibe you will create. In addition, we have included some valuable tools to help you: a comprehensive Materials List (shopping list) and a Critical Path (timeline/to do list) to keep you right on track.

You'll find the following terms, notations, and references in the plans:

❖ **Builder's Notes** | Our notes to you calling for your input.
❖ **Architect's Notes** | Our notes to you highlighting some insider's secrets.
❖ **Partybluprints Picks** | The products we purchased for our parties. You always have the ability to make your own selections; we just wanted to give you the benefit of our research and development and experience. Visit www.partybluprintsblog.com and click on the "Book Links" category at the top of the home page for details on all our Partybluprints Picks and more.
❖ **Expert Commentary** | From Kirk Sprenger, Wine Expert and Proprietor of The Chappaqua Wine & Spirit Company, Chappaqua, N.Y. He provides his expert opinion and advice on our wine selections, and, in many cases, advises us on wine selections, pairings, and rules.
❖ **Behind the Bluprint** | Our party notes.
❖ **Materials** | Ingredients.
❖ **Structural Notes** | How to use your materials to build your party.

You have the inspiration and information at your fingertips—let the planning begin. Pick the Party Plan that gets you the most excited; and, remember "U" are the most important element in each set of bluprints.

BEHIND THE BLUPRINT
—OUR PARTY NOTES

THE WINE COUNTRY CRUSH PARTY PLAN WAS CREATED as a way for us to share our travels to Napa and Sonoma with guests in our home. Our travels have taken us to Napa and Sonoma more than once, but we'll never forget that first trip—we visited over ten wineries in just three days. Some people like to show pictures when they get home from a great vacation; we like to throw a party. Our experience was so special that we truly wanted to give our family and friends a taste of this amazing part of the world. We designed the party with a vibe that would transport our guests to Napa for the night through our menu, wine, and special touches. We have hosted this party numerous times in its entirety, but have also used the first section to host a wine tasting followed by "small plates" style dining, featuring our select cheeses, risotto, and chocolate. Guests at this party always "oo and aah" at the different courses, the wine tasting generates great conversation and sharing, and the aroma makes your mouth water. We love the spirit of this party and the beautiful and special region it represents. Our guests have always had a ball with the wine tasting, and the

Our own private party in the vineyards. Clockwise from top: Dawn, Arnie, Elizabeth, and Mark taste testing flights of sparkling wine.

menu for this party is one of our favorites. The heart of this menu was inspired by a very special lunch we shared with our husbands in the Peju Kitchen. To read about it, search "Our most exciting food experience" on our blog, www.partybluprintsblog.com.

Stimulate Your Senses

PARTYBLUPRINTS
WINE COUNTRY CRUSH

THE PARTYBLUPRINTS WINE COUNTRY CRUSH PAIRS A WINE TASTING with a harvest dinner to take your guests on a virtual journey to Northern California Wine Country. Your guests will feel swept away to the special place you have created for them. Together, you will celebrate the bounty of the harvest.

BUILDER'S NOTE: Although this plan is designed for eight, you can adjust the Materials List to accommodate more or fewer. Just remember, this is meant to be an intimate evening, so we don't recommend more than twelve, including the host(s).

VIBE
√ **Alive**
√ **Fresh**
√ **Communal**

YOUR ITINERARY

The menu starts your evening off with an exuberant glass of sparkling wine to celebrate your crush. Once your guests are relaxed and in the spirit, treat them to a select Napa and Sonoma wine tasting. Gather around your table with a few bottles of wine. Consider this selection of wines like a good box of chocolates. Although they are all different, each bottle holds the promise of a new discovery. Enjoy tasting and sharing this experience. The tasting not only provides the basis for lively discussion, but it will also focus your guests on sharing an appreciation for the fruits of the crush season in Northern California Wine Country. Following this robust wine tasting, Your guests will savor the opportunity to enjoy more wine paired with a special cheese course and a Harvest Dinner. Imagine working all day to harvest the grapes for the crush and then celebrating at day's end. It is the perfect meal to cozy up to with friends and a few bottles of spectacular wine. No packing, no logistics to figure out, no plane—just you and your friends sharing an experience. Simply follow our Party Plan designed for eight.

Review Party Plan

YOUR SET OF BLUPRINTS

THE PARTYBLUPRINTS WINE COUNTRY CRUSH is designed to be the ultimate communal experience. The sharing of the wine, food and spirit of another region is your ticket to a new and exciting destination. Your Party Plan, a thoroughly coordinated "bluprint," details the concept, design, materials, and methods. We've put all the essential information and helpful tools at your fingertips. Simply follow your set of bluprints (Party Plan) and start building your party now.

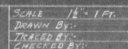

SCALE 1½" = 1 Ft.
DRAWN BY:-
TRACED BY:-
CHECKED BY:-

SKETCH SHEET.

DATE

PARTYBLUPRINTS = ARCHITECT
YOU = BUILDER

This Party Plan is your set of "bluprints"
for building your party.
You are the "U" in Partybluprints.

Your set of bluprints contains the following:

SCOPE & CORE ELEMENTS (Concept & Foundation)

SPECS (Party Components)

FOOTPRINT (Layout, Detailed Specs, Flow & Tablescape)

ARCHITECT'S NOTES (Insider's Tips)

MATERIALS LIST (Shopping List)

CRITICAL PATH (Timeline/To-Do List)

Virtual Trip Planner

WHO	Strictly Adults
WHAT	Wine Tasting & Harvest Dinner
WHERE	Your Home
WHEN	Late Afternoon/Early Evening
WHY	To Celebrate Anything!
HOW	Follow Bluprint

Scope & Core Elements
CONCEPT & FOUNDATION

YOUR EVENING IS A TRIBUTE TO NORTHERN CALIFORNIA WINE COUNTRY, featuring its wines and a meal inspired by its spirit (these are the core elements). Our Partybluprints Picks, which appear throughout the plan, identify our hand-selected products straight from this region. If you choose to order these products, you will not only be celebrating the region, but you will also be supporting their local economy—virtual tourism at its best. In effect, you and your guests are taking a virtual trip in the comfort of your home. You will connect with the heart of wine country by creating the spirit of the region. Are you ready to relax, release the wine, and relish the moment? An exciting virtual journey through Northern California Wine Country awaits you.

Specs
PARTY COMPONENTS

WE BELIEVE the most effective and enjoyable approach to entertaining is to start with a plan that stimulates all five senses. There are six key party components in every PARTYBLUPRINTS PARTY PLAN:

Invitations

Cocktails

Food

Music

Special Activities

Favors

The Specs section details the building materials and guidelines for each party component. Pay attention to all the components of your party and make sure they enhance, and do not detract, from one another. Consider this party a symphony for the senses: vision, palate, aroma, acoustics, and feeling. If you achieve the right balance, your guests' senses will be satisfied, which results in relaxed, happy guests and the perfect party environment!

Invitations

Ask your guests to join you on a trip to Northern California Wine Country to toast the bountiful harvest of this region and celebrate the promise of a new vintage. Your evening pays homage to the earth, so be down to earth and pen a personal note to each guest. Our suggestion for the contents of the invitation:

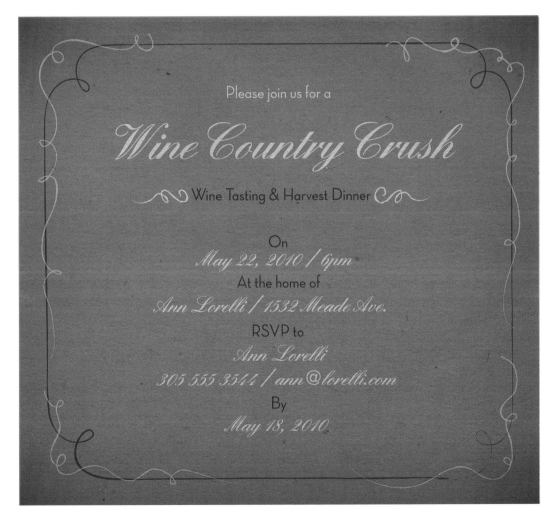

Please join us for a

Wine Country Crush

Wine Tasting & Harvest Dinner

On
May 22, 2010 / 6pm
At the home of
Ann Lorelli / 1532 Meade Ave.
RSVP to
Ann Lorelli
305 555 3544 / ann@lorelli.com
By
May 18, 2010

Partybluprints Pick: Water Pear Press Note Card Set featuring Napa Valley photos by wine country photographer, Nicholas Elias, Napa Valley Products, Napa, CA. You may choose to create invitations in your own style, which convey the vibe of your evening.

The Spirit of Wine Country

WHEN YOU FIRST CATCH A GLIMPSE of Napa or Sonoma County, the view literally takes your breath away. The mountains, with their sweeping and gentle slopes, meet at the bottom to form spectacular valleys where luscious gifts abound. The air is fresh, infused with subtle hints of flowers, fruit, vegetables, and other vegetation. The scent goes straight to your head and leaves you weak in the knees. The earth is rich and supple. You feel your feet leave their impression as you walk. The land, the gentle winds, the radiant sun, and the judicious rain combine to create an environment perfect for nurturing grapes, bountiful fruits and vegetables, olives, luscious landscapes, content animals, and passionate craftsmen. Given nature's bounty and their own undying passion, local artisans ardently craft their goods, which results in highly distinctive wines, cheeses, olive oils, and more.

The undisputed King of Napa and Sonoma is the wine. This region is optimal for growing grapes; the various microclimates produce some of the world's best red, white, and sparkling wines. By the time you are sitting at your first winery sipping a delicious taste of wine, your body instinctively relaxes as you celebrate the splendor of this world. Floating from winery to winery, removed from the outside world and surrounded by nature's beauty, you start to feel heady. Everything thrives in this region, including your spirit. The trick is to drink in the moment with all of your senses.

As the seasons come and go, the earth and its elements work in unison to prepare for the annual harvest which supports this region. The vineyards have been meticulously tended, and the plump grapes eagerly await "the crush." Depending upon the year's weather conditions, the grapes are ready anytime from September through October. Each vineyard's winemaker will make the call as to the exact date the grapes will be harvested and delivered for "the crush." The crush in Wine Country is a culminating and celebratory event.

Here are our
Partybluprints Picks for your
virtual trip menu.

Wine Country Crush

Menu

Cocktails

Black Olive Canapés
Paired with California Sparkling

Wine

WINE TASTING
Napa and Sonoma Chardonnay
and Cabernet Sauvignon

CHEESE COURSE
Cheese Selection with Assorted
Condiments/Accompaniments
Paired with California Chardonnay

Main Course

Harvest Salad
Risotto with Braised Beef Short Ribs
in Cabernet Sauce
Paired with California Cabernet Sauvignon

Dessert

Chocolate Truffles
Crush Cake

Cocktails

(Serves 8)

CALIFORNIA SPARKLING WINE

This evening is all about the wine. So welcome your guests with one that sparkles. With a glass of "bubbly" and a warm welcome into your home, any troubles of the day will slide right off, which puts your guests into the perfect state of mind to enjoy this exquisite evening.

Partybluprints Pick: Schramsberg Blanc de Blanc Sparkling Wine, Calistoga, Calif.

Materials
2 bottles California Sparkling Wine

Structural Notes
❖ Thoroughly chill sparkling wine.
❖ Fill each guest's glass ¾ of the way full.

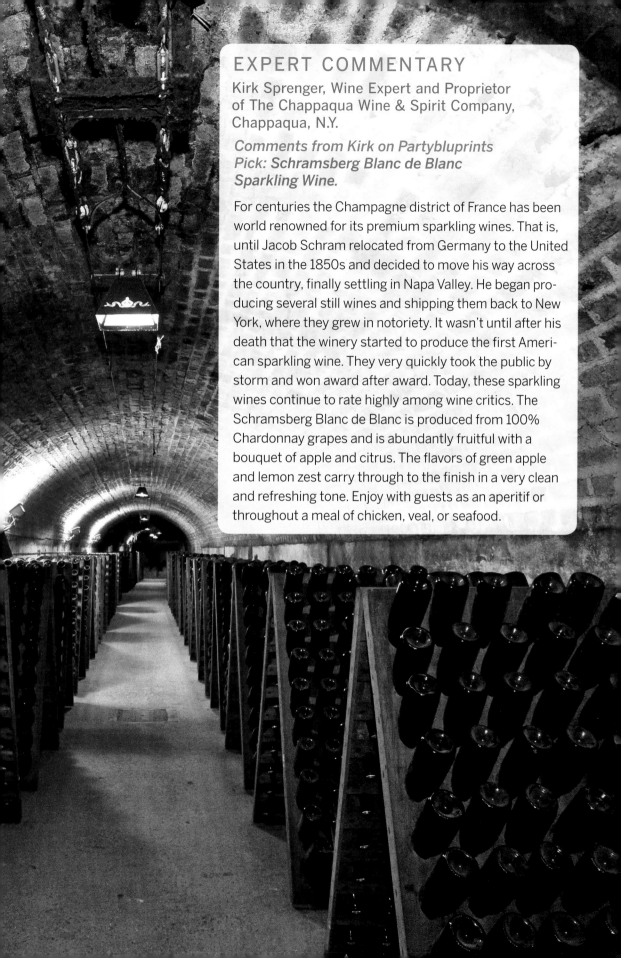

EXPERT COMMENTARY

Kirk Sprenger, Wine Expert and Proprietor of The Chappaqua Wine & Spirit Company, Chappaqua, N.Y.

Comments from Kirk on Partybluprints Pick: Schramsberg Blanc de Blanc Sparkling Wine.

For centuries the Champagne district of France has been world renowned for its premium sparkling wines. That is, until Jacob Schram relocated from Germany to the United States in the 1850s and decided to move his way across the country, finally settling in Napa Valley. He began producing several still wines and shipping them back to New York, where they grew in notoriety. It wasn't until after his death that the winery started to produce the first American sparkling wine. They very quickly took the public by storm and won award after award. Today, these sparkling wines continue to rate highly among wine critics. The Schramsberg Blanc de Blanc is produced from 100% Chardonnay grapes and is abundantly fruitful with a bouquet of apple and citrus. The flavors of green apple and lemon zest carry through to the finish in a very clean and refreshing tone. Enjoy with guests as an aperitif or throughout a meal of chicken, veal, or seafood.

AS A COMPLEMENT TO YOUR WELCOME COCKTAIL, offer your guests a few items they can "snack" on while waiting for the wine tasting to begin (FYI: there is no food served during the wine tasting, so now is your opportunity to take the edge off any hunger pangs). Light snacks include Black Olive Canapés, California smoked almonds, and champagne grapes.

Food
(Serves 8)

Black Olive Canapés

Black Olive Canapés pair perfectly with the sparkling wine and are a satisfying nibble for guests who arrive hungry.

Materials
2 large French baguettes
½ cup olive oil
12 oz. container cream cheese
6 oz. jar black olive tapenade
Kosher salt or coarse sea salt to taste

Structural Notes
❖ Preheat the oven to 400 degrees.
❖ Slice the bread on a slight angle into one-inch thick slices.
❖ Arrange sliced bread flat on baking pans in single layers.
❖ Lightly brush each slice with olive oil, sprinkle with the coarse sea salt.
❖ Bake ten to fifteen minutes, until golden brown and crunchy. Make sure they don't get too well done. Allow to cool completely. Store in an airtight container for up to four days.
❖ Mix cream cheese and olive tapenade until thoroughly combined.
❖ You may prepare and refrigerate up to six hours in advance.
❖ If prepared ahead, give the mixture a quick stir before serving.
❖ Top each crostini with mixture and serve on an attractive tray/platter.

As a little extra treat for your guests, serve California grown almonds and champagne grapes. This provides additional sustenance before the wine tasting.

Partybluprints Picks for small nibbles before wine tasting:
Black olive tapenade: Napa Tapas Black Olive Tapenade, Napa Tapas, Napa, Calif.
California grown smoked almonds, Napa Valley Products, Napa, Calif.
Optional: Champagne grapes. Check your local market for these "seasonal" delicate mini-bubbles in a bunch (that's what champagne grapes look like). They are not only delicious, but make a beautiful and interesting presentation.

Special Activities

WINE TASTING

NAPA/SONOMA WINE TASTING

A wine tasting makes for a dynamic evening for a tight knit group of friends or soon-to-be friends. The focus is on exploring and sharing wine in a relaxed and fun manner. Conversation will flow as easily as the wine.

This Partybluprints Napa/Sonoma Wine Tasting features two varietals, Chardonnay and Cabernet Sauvignon, from different microclimates within the same region. This region is known for producing some of the best Chardonnay and Cabernet Sauvignon in the world. After this tasting, you will agree.

From our travels through Napa and Sonoma, we selected a few of our favorite wines to feature in this wine tasting. The wines are equally matched; there is no unfair advantage. The tasting gives guests an opportunity to experience the outstanding qualities of two different types of wine. These Napa and Sonoma wines will go head to head in two different stand-offs, one featuring Chardonnay and the other starring Cabernet Sauvignon. Given your guests' preferences, favorites will emerge. All of the featured wines are memorable and special. Not only will your guests savor the evening, they will walk away with at least one (and probably more) new "go to" wines.

Partybluprints Picks for the Wine Tasting and Harvest Dinner Pairing:

California Chardonnays:
> *Chalk Hill, Estate Bottled, Sonoma*
> *Peju Estate, Napa Valley*
> *Grgich Hills, Napa Valley Estate Grown*
> *Miner Family Vineyards, Napa Valley*
> *Jordan, Sonoma*

California Cabernet Sauvignons:
> *Grgich Hills, Napa Valley*
> *Chalk Hill, Estate Bottled, Sonoma*
> *Whitehall Lane Reserve, Napa Valley*
> *Peju Estate, Napa Valley*

Materials
3 bottles Chardonnay
3 bottles Cabernet Sauvignon

Structural Notes

❖ Two hours before the Wine Tasting, chill the three bottles of Chardonnay. This is ample time for Chardonnay to reach its optimal temperature of forty-five degrees. Do not over chill the Chardonnays. If they are too cold, you will miss out on the true flavors of California Chardonnay. Contrary to widespread belief, quality California Chardonnay should not be served ice cold; this masks the flavors. Experiment with the Chardonnays and notice the difference in taste as they warm up. We actually enjoy it closer to room temperature rather than ice cold. See for yourself.

❖ One hour before the Wine Tasting, open the three bottles of Cabernet Sauvignon and allow them to breathe. This introduction of air to the wine "opens" the wine, resulting in the emergence of its true essence and flavor. If you have a decanter, decant your Cabernet by pouring it into the decanter and allowing it to breathe. Cabernet should be served at cellar temperature, fifty-five to sixty-five degrees.

❖ Set up your Wine Tasting Bar. If you do not have a bar, use a table, island, or counter large enough to accommodate a Wine Tasting Bar. If you are using a tablecloth, use a white tablecloth as a contrast against the color and clarity of the wine.

HOW TO SET UP A WINE TASTING BAR
THE WINE TASTING BAR ESSENTIALS

Materials

- ☐ 8 stemmed white wine glasses
- ☐ 8 stemmed red wine glasses
- ☐ 8 water glasses
- ☐ 6 bottles of wine (one of each of the wines you are featuring)
- ☐ A pitcher of still water, no ice—used to cleanse the palate in between wines.
- ☐ A dump bucket—an opaque pitcher/container used for dumping any unconsumed wine from the wine glasses. Do not use a clear container; no one wants to see the contents of the dump bucket.

Structural Notes

- ☐ Make a provision for the dirty glasses. Use a molded plastic bin (like the ones they keep glasses in at restaurants) to store dirty glasses out of the way until the next day.
- ☐ Offer wine crackers or plain grissini. This also serves to cleanse the palate in between wines.
- ☐ Provide "Wine Tasting Notes" for your guests. Make two copies of the "Wine Tasting Notes" from the form included with this plan, as there are six wines to taste. Fill in the specifics on your featured wines (e.g., the vineyard, the name and vintage of the wine, and any tasting notes you may want to include from Kirk's commentary below). You can also note the host and date of the party (e.g., The Smith's Wine Tasting, Sept. xx, 20xx).

  If you want to further personalize, include a personal note to your guests. Make sixteen copies (two for each guest)—they will appreciate the information on the wines they taste and can take it home as a great reference tool. Don't forget to provide pens.

- ☐ Optional: Make copies of Kirk's Commentary and Wine Tasting Basics for your guests for their information and future reference.

- ☐ Softly light this area with a combination of dimmed light and candlelight so your guests can see the color and clarity of the wines. Stick to scentless votive candles, as fragrance can detract from the tasting and smell is an important component of the wine tasting experience. Also, keep your candlelight out of the direct area of the wine tasting as there will be a lot of movement in this area.

WINE TASTING DIRECTIONS

Welcome your guests to the wine tasting and invite them to find a spot at the Wine Tasting Bar.

- ☐ Start by tasting the "lightest" varietal, Chardonnay, and then move to the Cabernet Sauvignon.
- ☐ Remember, there is a lot of wine to taste, so pour light during the tasting with a one-ounce pour per glass. Let your guests know that you will be serving a select Chardonnay with the cheese course and a select Cabernet with dinner, but don't reveal your selections until after the tasting is completed.

- ☐ Inform your guests that it is completely acceptable to take a sip and then discard the remainder in the dump bucket.

- ☐ Let your guests set the pace. If they are savoring each sip, do not hurry them. Likewise, if they are anxious to try the next wine, you can move things along.

- ☐ After tasting the first Chardonnay, direct your guests to dump their wine in the dump bucket, and then pour a splash of the next wine into their wine glasses. Direct your guests to coat their glass with this wine and then dump it. This prepares the glass for the next wine. (FYI: If you use water to rinse the glass, the next wine will be diluted by the water.) This is a great tip from Kirk. The tip not only makes you look professional, but also allows for optimal tasting of each wine. Our guests were very appreciative of this thoughtful extra step.

- ☐ Continue this pattern until all the wines have been tasted.

- ☐ Conclude the wine tasting by asking your guests to "cleanse" their glasses with the wine you have selected to serve with the cheese course and move the party into the area where your cheese course is presented.

- ☐ Make sure your guests keep track of all their wine glasses. At the conclusion of the wine tasting, after they have filled their glass with wine for the cheese course, have your guests locate their seat at the table and deposit their other two glasses. This assures their glassware is ready and waiting for them for dinner. If you prefer, you may preset the dining table with a set of glassware and have your guests leave their glasses at the Wine Tasting Bar.

BUILDER'S NOTE: For your wine tasting you will need to select three Northern California Chardonnays and three Cabernets. We list four to five of each varietal in the event that availability or cost is a factor. Again, if you're looking for a different price point, consult with a trusted wine expert and ask for something similar in your price range. If you have not established a relationship with a local wine proprietor, seek out some experts by visiting wine shops in your area. Wine experts can be an excellent resource and help you to explore your preferences. Remember to select two bottles of your favorite Chardonnay for the Cheese Course and four bottles of your favorite Cabernet for the Harvest Dinner.

EXPERT COMMENTARY

Kirk Sprenger, Wine Expert and Proprietor
of The Chappaqua Wine & Spirit Company, Chappaqua, N.Y.

Comments from Kirk on Partybluprints Picks: **Northern California Chardonnay and Cabernet.**

For those who have traveled the California wine country, the memories of the high rolling hills and depths of the valleys can almost be surreal. For those who have not yet visited the grape growing region of the gold coast, close your eyes and picture an ocean of hills and fields engulfed with grape vines beautifully terraced and pruned in the utmost immaculate conditions, rows and rows lined up in perfect harmony, soaking in the rays of the afternoon sun. These clusters of grapes and the terrain in which they grow can seem to meld into one. However, there are many microclimates that exist and can take two seemingly identical grapes and yield two very different wines in the bottle. Napa Valley alone has fourteen such sub-regions. So many factors influence the final product. The story begins with the soil; mineral, gravelly, or volcanic, each impart certain flavors, such as earthiness, and also make for a hearty root stock. Clay and sandy soils tend to impart lighter and more subtle flavors and are also more accommodating to less hearty varietals. Total sunlight will give a grape its fruitfulness and determine its depth and character. Basic geography tells us that the hills facing east will get less sun factors than those facing west. This also plays into how much warmth and/or cold the vines will be exposed to during the growing season. Certain varietals, such as Pinot Noir, tend to thrive in warm days and cooler nights, whereas, Cabernet Sauvignon and Merlot prefer the hot days and warm nights.

After the growing season and harvest, the final determining factor for a particular varietal is what the winemaker chooses to impart. Typically, his use of oak or stainless steel vats for the fermenting process will lend to the wines crispness or creaminess

WINE TASTING BASICS
By Kirk Sprenger
The proper way to assess a wine is by:

SIGHT Hold the wine in your glass at about a forty-five degree angle against a light surface. Check not only its color, but also its clarity. For a young wine especially, you want to make sure that it has a more brilliant clarity. By swirling the wine in the glass and allowing it to drift down the sides, you can see the appearance of "legs." This is the glycerin in the wine and indicates its depth of body.

SMELL Again, swirl the wine in the glass, and as it is still swirling get your nose into the glass and smell its fragrances. This is known as the "nose" or the bouquet. Take your time doing this. The more you swirl, the more air you will draw into the glass to release the essences of the wine. As the air mixes with the wine a chemical reaction occurs; this allows the scents and flavors to emerge. Close your eyes, if necessary, and mentally identify the components that you smell. These are the components that you then want to look for when you taste the wine.

TASTE Take in a moderate amount of wine into your mouth and start by gently swishing the wine around to all parts of your mouth. It is important for the wine to come into contact with all areas because each part of the mouth picks up different characteristics, such as acidity, sweetness, tannins of texture and also determines whether it will have the toasty quality of the oak barrel or the clean vibrancy of the steel. For this the winemaker looks at the harvest with which he has to work. As one tastes a white wine, perhaps for an opening course of various cheeses, the depth and flavors should be harmonious and complementary. If enjoying a light and delicate cheese such as Humboldt Fog, Purple Haze or Lamb Chopper, try complimenting it with a soft style of Chardonnay from Sonoma, such as Jordan or Chalk Hill. Both of these choices show just a subtle hint of oak that accents the fruit and hints at the underlying flavors of vanilla and pear. If enjoying a more hearty cheese, such as Roquefort or Stilton, head in the direction of one of these Napa Valley favorites, Miner Family, Peju or Grgich Hills. The longer exposure to oak fermentation has imparted a fuller body and more robust vanilla and spice character which will be an adjunct to your choice of cheese.

The same premise applies to the main course. Whether it's chicken, veal, beef, or lamb, pair the flavors of your food with your wine. Grgich Cabernet Sauvignon from Napa has a profusion of blackberry and licorice flavors with undertones of cedar—a perfect choice with a spiced Cajun dish or a hearty beef entrée. Chalk Hill (Sonoma) Cabernet Sauvignon and Whitehall Lane (Napa) Cabernet Sauvignon, though oaked, tend to show off a tremendous abundance of fresh berry and black cherry flavors while not denoting any sweetness levels. The hot days and warm nights of Whitehall Lane's vineyards let forth a burst of big ripeness in their wines. Matched up with a Porterhouse steak and grilled veggies or braised short ribs and the necessary accoutrements, these are perfect choices in reds. Peju in Napa, just south of Whitehall Lane, has a more westerly exposure and yields a very boastful Cabernet Sauvignon with a deep, rich body and a bit earthier, mineral quality. It's a great partner to leg of lamb or pot roast.

Upon my return from Napa and Sonoma, I, too, had a greater appreciation for a more meaningful food and wine pairing. This experience transferred to several of my clients. Now is the time to make your own pilgrimage to the wine country.

...

(the drying acids in a wine), oak, and fruit. Another method of tasting is to hold the wine in your mouth while slightly tilting your head forward and gently drawing in air through the wine, somewhat like sucking through a straw. This allows for more air contact, and, thus, a further release of the wine's essence. (Admittedly, this procedure does take practice.)

AFTERTASTE Yes, the sign of a good wine is the aftertaste. A wine that falls flat after it has been swallowed shows a lack of fruit. Fruity (the flavor in a wine) should not be confused with sweet (the residual sugar left in the wine). After all, wine is made from fruit and we do want to taste the fruit. A good aftertaste is known as "a long finish."

Partybluprints Addition to "The Wine Tasting Basics"

THE STORY Every bottle of wine has a story. The main elements of the story can be found right on the bottle: the name of the winery, the type of grape(s), where the grapes were grown (on the estate or by a farmer up the road), and the year the grapes were harvested. When you take the time to learn "the story" behind the bottle, you recognize and appreciate all the time, work, and passion that went into making your bottle of wine. This extra bit of "leg work" personalizes your tasting experience by allowing you to connect with the "roots" of your wine. This connection is sure to enhance your experience.

THE STORIES BEHIND THE WINE

Here are some stories we want to share about the wine and vineyards we selected for our tasting:

GRGICH HILLS: Our visit to Grgich Hills was a highlight of our trip, We were thrilled to have the opportunity to crush the grapes *I Love Lucy* style and learn about the place of Grgich Hills in wine history (their 1976 victory in a blind taste testing in France opened the door for Napa Valley in the wine world).

View from our rooms of the Whitehall Lane Vineyards.

Dawn and Elizabeth stomping the grapes at Grgich.

CHALK HILL: We enjoyed a jeep tour of the Chalk Hill property—yes, the grounds are that extensive and beautiful, certainly a sight to be seen—vineyards, organic gardens, guesthouses nestled in between. Although we did not have the opportunity to stay on premises during our visit, Kirk, our wine expert, and his wife, Cathy, were invited as guests to stay on the property—quite a special experience.

WHITEHALL LANE: When visiting Napa Valley, you can actually sleep in a cottage that is nestled in Whitehall Lane Vineyards. The Harvest Inn in St. Helena offers rooms with views of the vineyard and a few rooms where you can actually see the grapes from your bed—we can't think of a better way to connect emotionally with your wine than sleeping with it!

PEJU WINERY: The Peju Winery includes a very special feature—the Peju Kitchen. The chef creates recipes and dishes on site to pair with the Peju wines for an outstanding tasting experience. This was another highlight of our trip, as we found the Peju Kitchen to be a unique gathering place where wine and food meet to create magic!

WINE TASTING NOTES

Wine (Vineyard, Name, Vintage):

Aroma:

Taste:

Notes:

Wine (Vineyard, Name, Vintage):

Aroma:

Taste:

Notes:

Wine (Vineyard, Name, Vintage):

Aroma:

Taste:

Notes:

Food

CHEESE COURSE

Northern California cheese is garnering widespread attention, as its quality and taste rival the European cheese which many of us are familiar with and accustomed to serving. Although this region is primarily known for its wines, it is becoming recognized for its cheese, too. Share this insider's secret with your guests!

Oftentimes, a cheese course is enjoyed following a meal. We wanted to bring our cheese course to the forefront of the meal and present it as an opportunity to keep the momentum going following the wine tasting. Everyone will be excited following the wine tasting, so don't have them sit down at the table just yet. Sustain this excitement by allowing your guests to mingle in a relaxed and comfortable atmosphere as they enjoy tasting the various components of your cheese plate.

Your guests will enjoy exploring the tastes, textures, and combinations of this delectable cheese course while continuing the casual conversation ignited during the wine tasting. Tonight is all about tasting and trying new flavors, so encourage your guests again to be adventurous, this time with the cheese course.

Partybluprints Picks: Cypress Grove Chevre, Arcata, Calif.
> Humboldt Fog,
> Purple Haze Fresh Cherve, and
> Lamb Chopper.

ARCHITECT'S NOTE: After tasting a lot of California Cheese, we concluded that Cypress Grove Chevre, a Northern California cheese maker, was so outstanding and special that we could not pick just one of their cheeses. So we decided to share with you three different and fabulous cheeses, all from Cypress Grove. Each cheese, unique and special in its own right, should be tasted, savored, and admired for its originality.
Here are our tasting notes on the cheeses.
The Purple Haze *is so creamy and fresh, topped with unique and fresh flavors, you feel like you are eating on the farm.*
The Lamb Chopper *is extraordinary on its own, but is absolutely over the top with fresh honeycomb or even honey!*
The Humboldt Fog *is remarkable and distinctive; the combination of its signature edible vegetable ash and creamy white ripened center makes a statement.*

BUILDER'S NOTE: *For information on building your own cheese plate, visit www.partybluprintsblog.com, and search "build your own cheese plate" for the article.*

Food

CHEESE COURSE

Materials
16 oz. Humboldt Fog
10 oz. Fresh Chevre Purple Haze
16 oz. Lamb Chopper
4 fresh figs (if available)
2 fresh pears
3 large bunches red seedless grapes
2 squares fresh honeycomb or
   1 container honey
1 jar fig jam
1 large French baguette

Structural Notes

❖ Line two rectangular wooden platters/cutting boards with parchment paper to create the "plate." Arrange equal amounts of cheese (one ounce/guest), condiments, and fruit on each plate. Each should serve four guests.

❖ Cut the three cheese selections into individual portions. Do not cube the cheese; slicing it correctly (see below) yields more flavor. Your plates should be simple but elegant.

❖ Using a cheese knife, slice the Lamb Chopper as you would slice a sliver of cake. Do not lob off the end of the Lamb Chopper. The artisan spent too much time crafting this cheese for you to taste only a portion of it. When sliced correctly, you will get the full taste of the cheese—from the inside out. Once you have cut the slivers, slice them in half horizontally for individual-sized portions.

❖ Slice the Purple Haze into individual-sized wedges, like a serving of cake. This fresh chevre is extremely soft and becomes more difficult to cut and arrange as it warms up. Leave it in the refrigerator until ready to cut and plate.

❖ Slice the Humboldt Fog in the same manner.

❖ Serve the fig jam in a small bowl with a spoon.

❖ Place the honeycomb right on the plate; if using honey, serve it like the fig jam.

❖ Thinly slice the pear and fan it on the plate.

❖ Wash and dry the grapes before placing on the plate; you don't want water dripping off the grapes and ruining your cheese.

❖ If using fresh fig, slice into quarters.

❖ Thinly slice the baguette and serve alongside the cheese.

❖ Have your cheese plates waiting for your guests when they finish the wine tasting.

CHEESE COURSE TIPS AND TOOLS

> Always serve cheese at room temperature. If you remove the cheese from the refrigerator one hour before serving, the true flavor of the cheese will emerge.

> A cheese plate can be based upon many different themes: origin of milk (goat, sheep, or cow), region, texture, or cheesemaker (our theme for this party). The selection should contain cheeses of different textures and qualities. It is up to the cheesemaker to create a cheese with a distinctive taste and texture. Give your guests an opportunity to explore a wonderful range of tastes and textures in one cheese plate. Everyone is sure to have a favorite.

> Add some additional tastes and textures to your cheese plate by presenting some unexpected condiments such as Black Mission Fig Jam and fresh honeycomb (or honey) and accompaniments such as fresh figs (if available), pears, and grapes.

> Although the Black Mission Fig is the most common in California, it is not readily available year round. This fig has two seasons, a small crop is harvested for two weeks in June, and the larger second crop is harvested from August to November. If you choose to serve fresh figs with your cheese plates, serve them cut in quarters when ripe. Mission figs are ripe when they are shriveled up. For figs that aren't quite ripe, cut them in half, brush surface with olive oil and grill them cut side down just until they start to caramelize (when you see the surface and edges starting to brown, remove figs from the grill before they burn). In season, figs are always a great addition to a cheese plate.

> Keep it simple. Do not overload your cheese plate. It should be a presentation of a cheese plate, not a heaping "cheese tray"—choose your favorite condiments/accompaniments. This is an appetizer to whet your guests' appetites for dinner. A single serving of each cheese with a few condiments/accompaniments is enough of a taste, without being too much. Your guests should be hungry when they sit down to dinner.

Partybluprints Picks for Cheese Plate Condiments/Accompaniments:
> *Figs: If you can't find fresh figs locally, try ordering online from resources such as Local Harvest.*
> *Fig jam: We discovered a fig jam full of fig flavor in an easy to spread presentation, Black Mission Fig Jam, The Girl and the Fig Restaurant, Sonoma, Calif.*
> *Honeycomb/honey: Regional honeycomb from Marshalls Honey, American Canyon, Calif.*

BUILDER'S NOTE: Honeycomb (yes, honeycomb, not honey) is an unexpectedly fabulous complement to a cheese plate. You may need to help your guests navigate the honeycomb/cheese combination. They may not be sure if it is meant to be eaten and, if it is, how they should go about indulging. Set an example and cut off a piece of honeycomb and place it right on your piece of cheese. Our guests devoured this delicacy and were amazed by the flavor this combo creates. They were so excited that they ate actual honeycomb. This is good stuff, but when it sells out you'll have to rely upon another source or substitute regional honey, such as Napa Valley Natural Wildflower Honey, Valley Products, Napa, Calif. If you have trouble getting California honey or honeycomb, infuse a bit of your own local flavor and introduce your local honey/honeycomb to your cheese plates. Another option: The Savannah Bee Company makes some of the most amazing honeycomb and honey we have ever tasted.

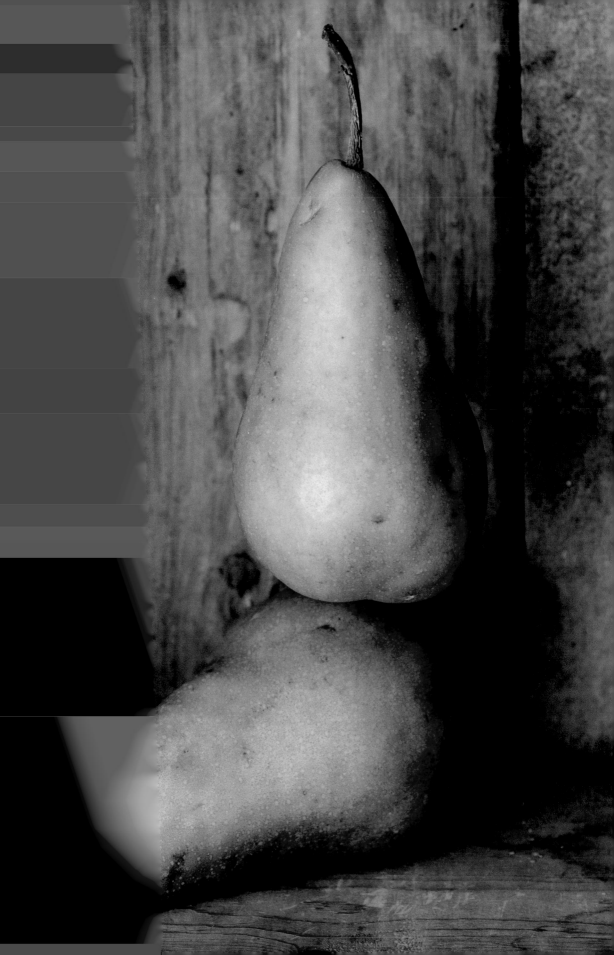

Food

MAIN COURSE

This Wine Country Crush Harvest Dinner celebrates nature's gifts in a Northern California style. Simplicity is a luxury afforded to this region's dishes due to the freshness and abundance of its plenty. Rustic cooking combined with fresh and artisanal ingredients creates an experience that will leave you and your guests feeling like you have been transported to a cool, starry wine country evening.

This meal pays tribute to a region and the hands that farm its land. All hands are at work, dawn to dusk, during the harvest and the crush. Consequently, no one is available to spend all day preparing a meal. In this spirit, bring your guests to the table for a meal reminiscent of dinner on the farm after a long "harvest" day.

We went back to the basics with fresh produce for a simple, yet stellar, harvest salad and a slow cooked supper, layered with so many flavors your guests will savor every bite. We added our twist on the basic starch—the risotto. It is the perfect partner for the beef. The combination is outstanding and will leave your guests dying to lick their plates. Finally, since we are celebrating "the crush," wine is an ingredient in every dish. Cheers!

Food

Harvest Salad

Start the meal with a refreshing salad that cleanses the palate. The red leaf lettuce provides a mild sweet basis for the slightly tart pomegranate, rustic shaved Parmigiano Reggiano, and hearty walnuts. We've included shaved fennel in this salad, not only because it tastes clean, but also because it's a natural digestive in case any of your guests overindulged in the cheese course.

Partybluprints Pick for Olive Oil and Red Wine Vinegar: Round Pond Italian Varietal Olive Oil and Red Wine Vinegar, Napa, Calif.

Materials
1 cup Round Pond Italian Varietal Olive Oil
½ cup Round Pond Red Wine Vinegar
1 lemon, juiced
½ tsp. fresh cracked pepper
½ tsp. sea salt
2 heads red leaf lettuce, washed and dried
1 fennel bulb, quartered and thinly sliced
2 pomegranates, seeded or 1 container pomegranate seeds
½ cup shaved Parmigiano Reggiano
½ cup chopped walnuts

Structural Notes
❖ In a jar or cruet, mix thoroughly dressing ingredients (olive oil through sea salt).
❖ In a large salad bowl, combine lettuce and fennel.
❖ Cover and refrigerate.
❖ If using a whole pomegranate, cut open and remove seeds. Refrigerate seeds separately until adding to salad.
❖ When ready to serve, toss lettuce and fennel. Shake dressing thoroughly and lightly dress salad. Sprinkle with pomegranate seeds, walnuts, and Parmigiano Reggiano.

Fresh Bread and Olive Oil

Serve fresh rustic style bread as a complement to this hearty meal. Further, treat your guests to some liquid gold, aka olive oil, from California. We discovered a beautiful haven at Round Pond Estate in Napa Valley, where the olives are picked from the estate's olive trees in the morning and pressed that same afternoon. The freshness of the olives is captured in this exquisitely bottled olive oil; it's extremely smooth and pleasing to the palate.

Food

(Serves 8)

RISOTTO TOPPED WITH BRAISED
BEEF SHORT RIBS IN CABERNET WINE SAUCE

There are several reasons this dish was a hands-down must for this
Harvest Dinner. These braised beef short ribs have the deep, rich flavors
that you can only get from slow cooked comfort food; it's even better
when prepared ahead, so make it the day before your party! Secondly,
served atop creamy risotto, this elegantly presented hearty meal is a
soul mate for the California Cabernet. Your guests will not know which
to savor, the meal or the wine! Finally, braising promotes economic and
environmental sustainability by making a "lesser" cut of beef absolutely
delectable and desirable. This issue is near and dear to many of the
farmers and wine producers in California Wine Country.

BRAISED BEEF SHORT RIBS
IN CABERNET SAUCE

These servings are not huge. They are meant to be savored
as a topping to the Risotto.

Materials
4 lbs. natural beef short ribs, cut English style, 1 ½ inch thick and trimmed
Sea salt and cracked black pepper, to taste
Olive oil, as needed, to coat the bottom of the pot for browning the beef
2 medium onions, peeled and roughly chopped
5 cloves garlic, peeled, roughly chopped
2 bay leaves
24 sprigs fresh thyme (8 for braising and 16 for garnish)
1 bottle Cabernet Sauvignon wine (don't cook with wine you wouldn't drink)
6 cups beef stock

Food

Structural Notes

- Using a nine-quart braising pot, add just enough oil to cover the bottom. Heat the oil over medium heat.
- Pat ribs dry and season ribs with sea salt and pepper. When the oil is hot, add the ribs.
- Brown all four sides of each rib. Remove ribs from the pot. Pour off most of the fat in the pot, leaving just enough to coat the bottom of the pan. Also, leave the nice brown bits at the bottom of the pan; they will create rich flavor in the sauce.
- Preheat oven to 350 degrees.
- With the small amount of oil and fat left in the pan, sauté onions and garlic for approximately fifteen to twenty minutes, just until onions are translucent, but not brown. Stir in the wine, bay leaves, and thyme. Boil the liquid mixture to reduce to half its original volume.
- Return the ribs to the pot and add enough stock to just cover the meat. Bring to a boil on the stovetop, cover tightly, and transfer to the preheated oven.
- Braise for three to four hours. The ribs are done when the meat is tender and just begins to fall off the bone.
- Remove meat from the pot and cool.
- Strain the remaining liquid into a container and refrigerate overnight.
- When the meat is cool, you can remove it from the bone and cut off the excess fat and tendons that hold the meat to the bone. Leave large chunks of meat; don't completely shred the beef. Cover meat and refrigerate.
- The next day remove the solid fat that has formed on the top of the sauce. This is the best way to separate and remove the fat. If you separate the fat when the sauce is warm, you are apt to lose a good portion of your sauce.
- One hour before serving, return the sauce and the ribs to your clean braising pot, cover and heat in a preheated 300-degree oven for an hour.

ARCHITECT'S NOTE: (1) The pot is important! It is important to both brown and braise the meat in the same pot so that the flavors left behind by the browning are included in the braised meat and sauce. Your pot must be large enough to hold four pounds of short ribs and all the liquid required for braising. Further, it must be a heavy-duty ovenproof pot, which provides for even cooking, with a lid that seals in the moisture. This is necessary for tenderizing the meat and preparing the sauce. (2) The beef should be made ahead of time (up to two days is great). The flavors are deep, rich and more complex if the beef "sits" a day or two. Since you are reheating the meat, you will still have that delicious aroma in your home before you serve this meal to your guests. The bonus is that you make it ahead of time, leaving you one less thing to do while you are entertaining your guests.

Risotto

We recommend using the following method to get a "jump start" on preparing the risotto. This method saves you from standing at the stove for twenty-five minutes and stirring while your guests wait for you. Ordinarily, we might avoid recommending such a dish for a dinner party; however, the risotto is the perfect companion to the braised beef short ribs and is definitely worth the ten minutes of final preparation.

Materials

3 tbsp. olive oil
4 medium shallots, diced
7 ½ cups chicken broth (½ cup extra
   if needed in final preparation)

2 ¼ cups Arborio rice
1 ¼ cups dry white wine
1 tsp. sea salt
1 ¼ cups freshly grated
   Parmigiano Reggiano

Structural Notes

❖ Set aside 2 ½ cups chicken broth for use in final preparation of risotto.

❖ In a saucepan, heat five cups chicken broth, cover, and keep warm on low heat.

❖ In a six-quart saucepan, heat oil over medium heat. Add shallots and sauté until tender, about ten minutes. Add Arborio rice to the shallots, mixing well until rice is lightly toasted.

❖ Stir in the wine and continue stirring until it is almost entirely absorbed.

❖ Add ½ cup of heated chicken stock to the rice mixture, and constantly stir until the rice absorbs the broth. Continue this process until you have stirred in five cups of broth.

❖ Pour rice into a shallow baking dish, cover, and refrigerate.

❖ Thirty minutes before serving risotto, remove from refrigerator and bring to room temperature.

❖ Heat remaining 2 ½ cups chicken broth in your risotto pan. Add partially prepared risotto to the chicken stock and stir until absorbed.

❖ Temporarily remove risotto from the heat and cover while you finish getting your guests to the table and serving the salad.

❖ While guests are finishing up their salad, return risotto to a medium heat and stir until risotto is piping hot and the correct consistency.

❖ The risotto should be creamy, not soupy; test by putting a spoonful on a plate. If a puddle of liquid forms, continue cooking and stirring until creamy. If the risotto is dry, add some additional warm broth until it's the correct consistency.

❖ Remove from heat and stir in Parmigiano Reggiano cheese.

❖ For an elegant presentation, place two spoonfuls of risotto on the center of each plate and make a well in the middle. Neatly place a small serving of Braised Beef Short Ribs in the well and spoon a tablespoon or two of the Cabernet sauce over the beef. Do not douse the dish with sauce.

❖ Garnish with thyme (form an X using two sprigs). Serve immediately.

❖ Cover remaining amount to keep warm for anyone who wants seconds.

❖ The initial serving amount should not overwhelm. As guests finish their servings, offer seconds.

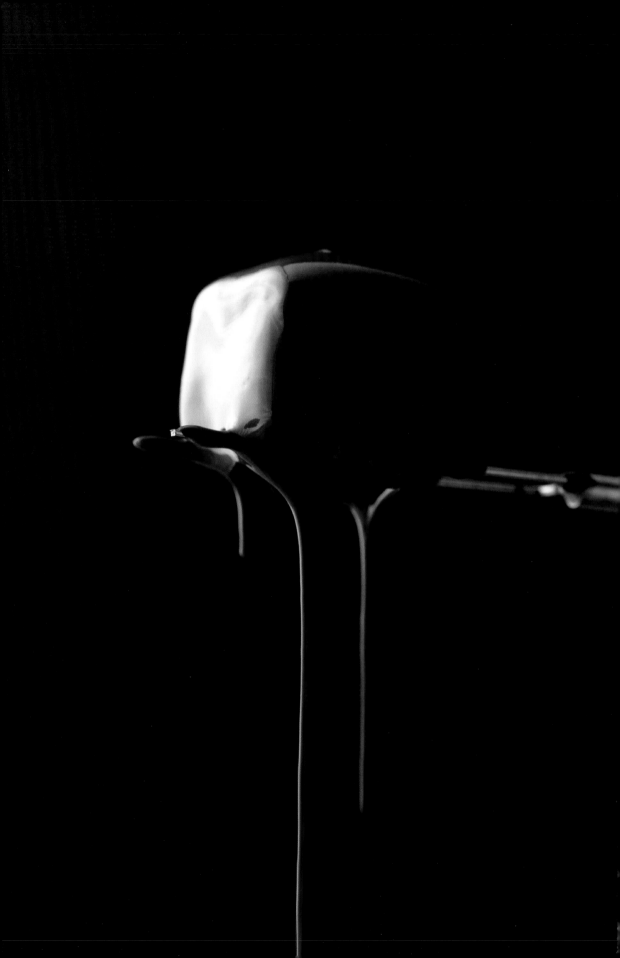

Food

DESSERT

WINE COUNTRY CHOCOLATES

In lieu of an after-dinner drink, serve chocolate truffles infused with wine. Chocolatiers are pairing wine and chocolate in the form of chocolate truffles. Serve these decadent morsels while preparing the main dessert. Your guests will be surprised to discover that these truffles contain something special—more wine!

Partybluprints Pick: Wine Country Chocolates, Glen Ellen, Cailf. Local wines are used to infuse ganache filling to create a perfect union of two of our all-time favorites, chocolate and wine. When we visited the shop, we saw these truffles being hand-dipped, just like in "the old days."

Materials
16–24 chocolate truffles

Structural Notes
❖ Arrange truffles on an attractive tray.
❖ After you have cleared the dinner dishes, serve the tray of truffles to your guests and ask them to indulge while you are plating the dessert.

COFFEE (OPTIONAL)

Serve dessert with a cup of coffee.

Materials
1 lb. coffee
Sugar
Cream

Structural Notes
❖ Set up coffee maker before party begins.
❖ Brew when serving dinner.

Food

CRUSH CAKE WITH PEARS AND CHOCOLATE SAUCE

Long before grapes were being planted in Napa, pear orchards were commonplace. *The San Francisco Chronicle* in 1923 actually described Napa pears as reaching "a fine state of perfection." Napa is also home to the only pear-focused gourmet condiment company in the country: A Perfect Pear of Napa Valley. As a tribute to this Napa fruit, we end our harvest dinner with our original Crush Cake recipe featuring the flavor of the perfect pear.

Partybluprints Picks: Pear Puree—The Perfect Puree of Napa Valley. Chocolate Pear Cabernet Sauce—A Perfect Pear of Napa Valley.

Materials
1 box of pound cake mix (plus ingredients needed per box instructions: eggs and milk)
2 oz. sour cream
4 oz. pear puree, thawed*
½ tsp. vanilla
2 pears
1 jar Chocolate Pear Cabernet Sauce

Structural Notes
❖ Preheat oven according to directions. Grease a loaf pan and set aside.
❖ Follow the mixing directions on the back of the cake mix box.
❖ Add in the sour cream, pear puree, and vanilla to the cake mix, and continue to follow the directions on the box.
❖ When the cake is cooked and cooled, cut one-inch slices.
❖ On a dessert plate, drizzle the Chocolate Pear Cabernet Sauce in a zigzag pattern across the bottom of dish and set the pound cake on top. Cut paper-thin slices of pear, dip outside edges of pear in chocolate and stick two standing up in each slice of cake. The pear and chocolate make a perfect pair!

ARCHITECT'S NOTE: The minimum order for Perfect Puree is three containers. You only need 4 ounces to make the cake, so you will have lots left over. You can use the puree to cook or make great drinks. Instead of ordering 3 containers of pear, try the white peach (for great Bellini Cocktails) and/or another flavor that interests you. You can also make your own pear puree.

Special Touches

Music

Create a music mix or playlist composed of Wine Country inspired music, such as "Jazz on the Vine" and Napa Valley Moonlight Serenade.

Partybluprints Pick: Partybluprints iTunes iMix, visit www.partybluprintsblog.com and click on "Book Links" category at the top of the home page for details. Reminder: you can also find all the links for the Partybluprints Picks here.

Special Activities

The Wine Tasting is the activity. We've spelled it all out for you in the Wine Tasting instructions. The only embellishment you may choose is a personalization of your guests' Wine Tasting Notes.

Favors

When you travel, it is customary to bring home an item you discovered on your trip. Send your guests home with a favor containing Wine Country Spirit.

Partybluprints Pick: Round Pond Mini Bottle Gift Set, Napa, Calif. Now that you've introduced your guests to the exquisite wonders of liquid gold and its partner, gift them a beautifully packaged gift box of Round Pond Olive Oil and Red Wine Vinegar to enjoy at home. As an alternative, you can purchase small glass bottles with a cork at your local craft, kitchen or dollar store and fill with California Olive Oil. Tie a note to the neck of the bottle and write a message of thanks or simply "Liquid Gold to go!"

Footprint

Layout & Detailed Specs

DESIGN BOARD:
VINEYARD ROSES, WOOD BARRELS,
VINEYARD GRAPES, AND WINE

THE INSPIRATION FOR THIS TABLESCAPE comes from wine country's bounty—its fruit, flora, and the colors of its "crush" season landscape. As you drive up and down the highways and lanes that wind through Napa and Sonoma Valley, you are struck by the perfectly straight rows of vines. During the "crush" season, these rows are bursting with plump and juicy grapes. Accentuating each row are roses lining the edges of the vineyards. **Replicate these elements in your tablescape:**

> Flowers | A blend of rustic and simple elements elegantly presented demonstrates you can transform your appreciation for natural beauty into a visually stunning masterpiece. This centerpiece represents the rows of vines in the vineyard during the crush season as it runs down the length of the table. Its low and long arrangement allows everyone at the table to enjoy its beauty while allowing for easy conversvation across the table.

> Wood | Use placemats instead of a tablecloth on a wooden table to establish a rustic feel and feature the beauty of natural wood. Wood chargers are the ideal foundation for each place setting. They are a substantial anchor for the white dishes and add warmth and richness to the tablescape.

> Linens | Be inspired by the palette of your harvest flowers. Match your table runner and placemat to a harvest color in the floral arrangement. We chose to match the linens to the Orange Wheat Celosia.

> Wine | Give the wine a place of honor on your table and anchor both ends of your centerpiece with a bottle of wine.

> Grapes | Every vineyard must have grapes, the perfect accent to your place cards.

> Candlelight | Dot your landscape with pillar candles and votive candles.

Flow

THE FLOW OF YOUR EVENING should be relaxed and casual as you move your guests from one area to the next. Your dining room table will be the final destination of your trip, but before you get there, you and your guests have a few stops to make as you explore and discover.

Structural Notes

> Walk around the inside of your home to determine the flow of your party. Scout out the site of your various stations/"stops."

> The location of your stations will determine the flow of your party. The goal is to provide areas where people can congregate and mingle. Guests should be able to flow effortlessly from one station to another and help themselves at the various stations:

 1. Welcome Station: This station requires fluted glasses, California Sparkling Wine, cocktail napkins, and appetizers. Accessorize this area simply with votive candles, a dish of champagne grapes if available, and some lavender (Northern California is a big lavender supplier) in a pretty, petite vase. If lavender is unavailable, use a few leftover blooms from the centerpiece to create a petite arrangement.

 2. Wine Tasting Bar: Refer to all-inclusive wine tasting instructions.

 3. Cheese Course: The third station will be the hub of the pre-dinner/post-wine tasting conversation. Make it easy for your guests to try different combinations of cheeses and toppings by selecting a space that allows for easy and ample access to the plates. To continue nature's fruit and flora theme, place a small floral arrangement by each cheese plate, along with some votive candles. These arrangements can be made from the leftover flowers used to make the centerpiece for the dining table.

 4. Main Dining Table.

> Determine if you need to rearrange any furniture or need additional tables/chairs, etc.

Tablescape

THE LONG AND WINDING harvest floral centerpiece is the focal point of your table. Its long and narrow composition allows for easy conversation across and around the table, while still making its presence known.

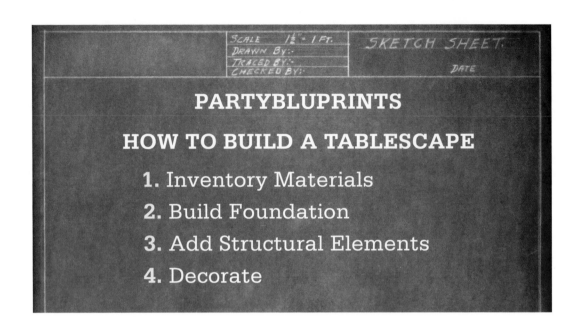

PARTYBLUPRINTS

HOW TO BUILD A TABLESCAPE

1. Inventory Materials

2. Build Foundation

3. Add Structural Elements

4. Decorate

Tablescape Materials List

INCLUDED IN COMPREHENSIVE MATERIALS LIST

USE THESE MATERIALS TO CREATE YOUR TABLESCAPE:

> Midnight Magic Roses

> Red Viburnum Berry branches

> Lemon leaves

> Green Tricillium

> Orange Wheat Celosia

> Bright green Pompom Mums

> Long and narrow wooden containers

> White pillar candles

> Small wooden cutting boards

> Table runner

> Cloth placemats

> Matching cloth napkins

> Wooden chargers

> White dishes

> Utensils

> Water glasses

> Wine glasses

> Wine corks

> Place cards

Structural Notes

1. INVENTORY YOUR MATERIALS

Take your Materials List (included at end of the plan), and go on a scavenger hunt in your home to determine what materials you have and what you need. Place items you have in a staging area near your table.

2. BUILD FOUNDATION

Clean table. Place runner down center of table.

3. ADD STRUCTURAL ELEMENTS

Floral centerpieces | Start with wooden rectangular containers; we used vintage wooden cream-cheese boxes. Check your local craft store for wooden rectangular containers or you may use other rectangular containers; just make sure the color will be camouflaged by the flowers.

If using wooden containers, insert a "watertight" liner/container to ensure the container safely holds the water before starting arrangement. Arrange the containers almost end to end down the length of the table (if someone will be seated at the heads of the table, leave room

for a place setting at each end). Line the perimeter of the containers with lemon leaves and Red Viburnum Berry. This has a dual purpose: 1) to camouflage the containers (you want your centerpiece to look as if it grew on the table), and 2) to create the look of the leaves on the grapevines. Cut the stems of your flowers to fit the height of the containers; always err on the side of cutting them too long, since you can always cut them shorter. Continue the natural "growing" look of your centerpiece as you add the next layer to the inside perimeter. Prepare the containers for the roses by filling them with Green Tricillium, Orange Wheat Celosia, and bright green Pompom Mums; randomly alternate the flowers. Fill containers halfway with water to cover bottoms of stems. Finally, add Red Roses; they should stand upright as you weave them into the center of the arrangement. Make sure to offset them slightly from one another so they look like they grew there and were not "lined up." We chose a magnificent variety of red roses, Midnight Magic. Their rich hue and

Set the place setting as shown in the photo. Fold each napkin in thirds lengthwise. Lay the napkin lengthwise between the main course dish and the salad plate. Garnish the salad plate with a handful of grapes, two lemon leaves, and a handmade wine cork place card holder. To make the place card holder, use a knife to make a slice along the length of a wine cork. Use the slit to hold the place card.

velvety texture are reminiscent of the wine. If your local florist can't order these flowers, ask for a suitable alternative, but keep the colors the same—deep red, orange, and green. These colors mimic those of the wine country landscape during the crush season.

Candlelight and Wine | Anchor each end of the centerpiece with a small cutting board (an olive wood board is beautiful, but any presentable cutting board will do). On each cutting board, place two bottles of the Cabernet you are serving with dinner and a pillar candle. Light the candle when you sit down to dinner and dim the lights in your dining room. Traditional Harvest Dinners commence at sunset or twilight. If you feel you need additional candlelight, dot the length of the table with votives to represent the starry night.

4. DECORATE

Place Settings | A sense of festivity should emanate from your dinner table as your guests sit down to celebrate the harvest of the season. For each place setting, use a solid placemat and matching napkin. We chose to match the linens to the Orange Wheat Celosia, which is in the burnished golden-brown family, used in the centerpiece. If you cannot find this color, we suggest a natural color that enhances the centerpiece. Using placemats instead of a tablecloth on a wooden table establishes a rustic feel and features the beauty of natural wood. Wood chargers, oversized plates meant for accessorizing not eating, are the ideal foundational piece for each place setting. They offer the perfect contrast to white dishes, while adding warmth and richness to the overall tablescape.

PARTYBLUPRINTS RULE OF GOOD MEASURE

"Always inventory materials before purchasing."

1. Search your home, including storage, for materials.

2. Use your imagination—repurpose items.

3. Borrow.

Architect's Notes

INSIDER'S TIPS

1 **This is not your typical dinner party**, it is an event. We suggest the following timing: begin at 6 p.m. to avoid being rushed, cocktails 6–6:30 p.m., Wine Tasting 6:30–7:30 p.m., Cheese Course 7:30–8:15 p.m., and Harvest Dinner 8:15–???

2 **Do not delay starting your wine tasting** due to late guests. Start at the appointed time, thirty minutes into the party or earlier if all your guests are prompt and have enjoyed a glass of bubbly. If guests arrive late, include them with the current wine you are tasting. When the wine tasting is completed, they can go back and taste what they missed.

3 **Near the end of the Cheese Course**, excuse yourself to finish the risotto, which will take about ten minutes. When you are done, cover it, remove from heat and leave it on the stove. Invite your guests to be seated at the dinner table.

4 **Place a few bottles of still and sparkling water** on the dining table for your guests and then pass them or pour them when everyone is seated.

5 **If you don't have a co-host**, ask one of your guests to help you throughout dinner (pour the wine and help you serve the courses). This lessens your time away from the table—your guests may become uncomfortable if you're gone too long.

6 **Using a table or counter** in the kitchen that can accommodate eight plates, lay out the plates for easy plating and serving.

7 **This entrée is served restaurant style**, not family style where everyone gets a huge helping. This is a rich meal and you want your guests to savor every last bite and leave them wanting a little more. You want your guests to feel satiated, not stuffed. Remember this evening is all about balance.

8 **Remember the "U" in Partybluprints** and add your special touches. Whether it is through your decorating, sharing your favorite Napa or Sonoma Chardonnay or Cabernet with your guests, or personalizing a favor for your guests with a "goodnight note," bring your "builder's inspiration" to your party.

Materials List

USE THE INCLUDED MATERIALS LIST as your inventory and shopping list all in one. Simply make a copy and check off items you have before doing any shopping. Then, as you shop, continue to inventory items until all materials are "in-house."

Be efficient and keep an updated copy of your list with you whenever you go shopping and update it in real time. This avoids over purchasing and last minute impulse shopping (we like to call it "panic purchasing"), resulting in unnecessary stress and expenditures.

Critical Path

FOLLOW THE INCLUDED CRITICAL PATH to manage your time and tasks so you are not overwhelmed or unprepared for your guests. This guide combines your to-do list and timeline for efficient and effective preparation and execution. We've removed the guesswork and streamlined the process. If you stick to the Party Plan, you can prepare everything ahead of time and be a guest at your own party. What a sweet reward for a job well done!

PARTYBLUPRINTS WINE COUNTRY CRUSH
MATERIALS LIST
SHOPPING LIST FOR 8

- ☐ 2 bottles California Sparkling Wine
- ☐ 1 container California smoked almonds
- ☐ 1 container champagne grapes (if available)
- ☐ 3 large fresh French baguettes
- ☐ 1 (12 oz.) container cream cheese
- ☐ 1 (6 oz.) jar black olive tapenade
- ☐ 1 package grissini or wine crackers
- ☐ 3 different bottles Chardonnay (see recommendations for Wine Tasting)
- ☐ 2 bottles Chardonnay (for Cheese Course)
- ☐ 3 different bottles of Cabernet Sauvignon (see recommendations for wine tasting)
- ☐ 4 bottles Cabernet Sauvignon (for dinner)
- ☐ Cooking wine: (Don't use a wine you wouldn't drink, choose a great value wine) 1 bottle Chardonnay (Risotto material) 1 bottle Cabernet Sauvignon (Braised Beef Short Ribs material)
- ☐ 4 bottles still water (you can use tap water)
- ☐ 2 bottles sparkling water
- ☐ 1 (16 oz.) Humboldt Fog cheese
- ☐ 2 (5 oz.) Fresh Chevre Purple Haze cheese
- ☐ 1 (16 oz.) Lamb Chopper cheese
- ☐ 4 fresh figs (if available)
- ☐ 4 fresh pears

- ☐ 6 large bunches red seedless grapes
- ☐ 2 squares fresh honeycomb or 1 container honey
- ☐ 1 jar fig jam
- ☐ 2 loaves fresh rustic style bread
- ☐ 1 bottle Round Pond Olive Oil
- ☐ 1 bottle Round Pond Cabernet Red Wine Vinegar
- ☐ 1 lemon
- ☐ coarse sea salt
- ☐ fresh cracked black pepper
- ☐ 2 heads red leaf lettuce, washed and dried
- ☐ 1 fennel bulb
- ☐ 1 container pomegranate seeds, if not available use 2 pomegranates, seeded
- ☐ Parmigiano Reggiano: 1 ¼ cup grated and ½ cup shaved
- ☐ ½ cup walnuts, chopped
- ☐ 4 lbs. natural beef short ribs, cut English style, 1 ½ inch thick and trimmed
- ☐ 2 medium onions
- ☐ 5 cloves garlic
- ☐ 2 bay leaves
- ☐ 1 bunch fresh thyme (need 24 sprigs)
- ☐ 6 cups beef stock
- ☐ 4 medium shallots
- ☐ 8 cups chicken broth
- ☐ 2 ¼ cups Arborio rice
- ☐ 4 oz. pear puree

PARTYBLUPRINTS WINE COUNTRY CRUSH
MATERIALS LIST
SHOPPING LIST FOR 8

- [ ] 1 box Betty Crocker pound cake mix (may substitute other brand) + ingredients listed on box: eggs and milk
- [ ] 2 oz. sour cream
- [ ] ½ tsp. vanilla
- [ ] 1 jar Chocolate Pear Cabernet Sauce
- [ ] 16–24 chocolate truffles
- [ ] 1 lb. coffee, cream, sugar
- [ ] 1 dozen Midnight Magic Roses
- [ ] 2 branches Red Viburnum Berry
- [ ] 2 bunches lemon leaves
- [ ] 10 stems Green Tricillium
- [ ] 10 stems Orange Wheat Celosia
- [ ] 10 stems bright green Pompom Mums
- [ ] Long and narrow wooden containers that run ¾ the length of your table—you may substitute other containers from your local craft store, just make sure they are a color that is camoflaugued by the flowers
- [ ] 2 white pillar candles
- [ ] 2 small wooden cutting boards
- [ ] 1 table runner (measure your table to determine size)
- [ ] 8 cloth placemats
- [ ] 8 matching cloth napkins
- [ ] 8 wooden chargers
- [ ] 8 white dishes
- [ ] 8 sets of utensils
- [ ] 8 water glasses (if you set your table with both a red and white wine glass, your guests have the option to select their wine and use the other glass for water)
- [ ] 8 wine glasses (you may opt to set your table with both white and red wine glasses, if so double the number)
- [ ] 8 wine corks
- [ ] 8 place cards
- [ ] 8 champagne flutes
- [ ] Optional: 1 bunch fresh lavendar (if available)—to be used at Builder's discretion.
- [ ] Parchment paper
- [ ] 9 qt. braising pot
- [ ] Wine Tasting Essentials (see Wine Tasting Bar Essentials)
- [ ] 2 cheese boards/plates
- [ ] cheese knives (optional)
- [ ] 8 appetizer plates
- [ ] 8 cloth cocktail napkins
- [ ] votives and candles
- [ ] favors

PARTYBLUPRINTS WINE COUNTRY CRUSH
CRITICAL PATH
TIMELINE/TO-DO LIST

Requires Immediate Attention (at least three weeks in advance)

☐ Choose the date for your Partybluprints Wine Country Crush party.

☐ Create a guest list. Ask yourself as you consider your audience if you want to mix it up a little and make some introductions or invite a close circle of friends.

☐ Order note cards, then send out invitations at least two to three weeks in advance of date.

☐ Determine essentials you have in stock (stemware, dishes, flatware, etc.) and order/purchase what you need.

☐ Order materials online if you choose Partybluprints Picks or locate select local sources you will use. For perishable items, arrange for delivery a few days before the party.

☐ Start saving wine corks for the place card holders—you will need eight.

Two Weeks before the Party

☐ Order the wine.

☐ Speak to your florist and place an order for the flowers.

☐ Buy containers for the centerpiece.

The Week before the Party

☐ Inventory items for the party and purchase any items still needed.

☐ Determine location of your various stations. If extra seating/tables are needed, arrange to borrow from friends/family.

☐ Test your sound system and create your playlist or music mix.

☐ Prepare your Wine Tasting Notes.

One to Two Days before the Party

☐ Shop for any last minute items, i.e., perishables: fresh produce, meats, and flowers.

☐ Make the Braised Beef Short Ribs according to the recipe.

☐ Make the crostini and put in an airtight container.

☐ Print out the Menu included in this Partybluprints Party Plan, frame it and display it.

One Day before the Party

☐ Take some time to choose an outfit in which you look and feel fantastic!

☐ Prepare the floral arrangements and tablescape (if you want to hold off arranging roses until day of party, put in water and refrigerate to keep them at their freshest).

☐ Make the place card holders.

☐ Set dining table with runner, placemats, chargers, dishes, napkins, flatware, and place cards (decide if you will set stemware at place settings or have guests bring in their glasses from wine tasting).

- ☐ Make the Crush Cake.
- ☐ With a dry cloth, wipe any spots off your wine/water glass for the tasting (your guest will be examining the wine in the glass and water marks and spots on the glass will detract from the experience).
- ☐ Set up your stations/"stops": "Welcome," "Wine Tasting," and "Cheese Course" (tablecloths, flowers, dishes, glassware, and any non-perishable components).
- ☐ Remove the fat from the top of the sauce, put beef and sauce back in the cleaned braising pot.

Morning of the Party

- ☐ Start the day off on a good note; it's the day of your party!
- ☐ Designate a time to get yourself ready and stick to it.
- ☐ Have a cup of coffee or whatever gets you going and start the final preparations for your party!
- ☐ Purchase fresh bread.
- ☐ Prepare salad and refrigerate.
- ☐ Prepare vinaigrette.
- ☐ Prepare Risotto partially according to recipe.
- ☐ Chill sparkling wine.

Six Hours before the Party

- ☐ Finish setting the dining table and complete tablescape/centerpiece.
- ☐ Add flowers to other stations.

Four Hours before the Party

- ☐ Prepare cheese plates, cover and refrigerate.
- ☐ Make the topping for the crostini and refrigerate.

Two Hours before the Party

- ☐ Chill Chardonnay.
- ☐ Remember the "U" in Partybluprints and add your special touches.
- ☐ You followed the Partybluprints Party Plan and physically prepared the party. Now it's time to prepare you. Shower and dress in something that makes you feel great. Let the excitement of your party envelop you.

One Hour before the Party

- ☐ Do a final walk through of all your stations.
- ☐ Open the three bottles of Cabernet for the wine tasting.
- ☐ Top the crostini appetizers, arrange them on a serving dish, and cover them with plastic wrap. You can leave them out to bring to room temperature.
- ☐ Put reserved chicken broth for Risotto in saucepan and place on stove. Now all you will have to do is turn on the burner to heat when you are ready for the final preparation.

Thirty Minutes before the Party

- ☐ Put grissini/wine crackers in serving container and display on Wine Tasting Bar.

- ☐ Set out cocktail nibbles (Black Olive Canapés, almonds, and champagne grapes) for your guests to enjoy upon arrival.

Fifteen Minutes before the Party
- ☐ Start the music.
- ☐ Light candles.
- ☐ Take a walk around, admire your work, and feel the vibe.
- ☐ Pour yourself a glass of bubbly and toast yourself for a job well done.
- ☐ Right before guests arrive, remove Chardonnays for wine tasting from refrigerator to avoid being over chilled (do the same with the Chardonnay for the Cheese Course, remove from refrigerator thirty minutes before serving).

Thirty Minutes into the Party
- ☐ Remove cheese plates from refrigerator to warm to room temperature, but do not put them out at the Cheese Course station yet.
- ☐ Begin wine tasting.
- ☐ After the wine tasting is underway and everyone is enjoying, sneak away to put the cheese plates out for the upcoming cheese course.
- ☐ Remove Risotto from refrigerator to warm to room temperature.

Upon Conclusion of Wine Tasting
- ☐ Invite everyone to enjoy the cheese course with a glass of wine.
- ☐ Help yourself to some cheese, honeycomb, and other toppings to show guests how they might enjoy new tastes and new combinations.
- ☐ Open two bottles of Cabernet for dinner to allow them to breathe.
- ☐ Heat chicken broth for final Risotto preparation.
- ☐ Put the water and bread on the table.
- ☐ Reheat Braised Short Ribs on low heat in the oven.

Upon Conclusion of Cheese Course (allow forty-five minutes)
- ☐ Invite your guests to sit down at the dining table.
- ☐ Ask someone to pour wine while you toss and serve the salad course.
- ☐ While everyone is finishing up their salad, slip away to finish the Risotto—follow recipe.
- ☐ Ask for an assistant to clear the salad plates, and help plate and serve the entrée.
- ☐ Enjoy dinner!
- ☐ When clearing the dinner plates, begin brewing the coffee and serve chocolate truffles.
- ☐ Plate dessert (as per recipe) and serve with coffee.
- ☐ Don't forget to give your guests their favor as a reminder of a beautiful and special evening you just enjoyed.

BEHIND THE BLUPRINT —OUR PARTY NOTES

A NIGHT IN VENICE PARTY PLAN IS ONE THAT I (DAWN) HAD ALWAYS WANTED TO HOST. My husband and I went to Venice for our honeymoon. The water, lights and delicious food were magical, and I wanted to share that experience with everyone. A very special part of Venice life is food, and the locals have a unique way of relishing it. Cicchetti Bars are everywhere in Venice. Patrons of these bars enjoy tapas-style snacks and small glasses of wine called Ombra. I loved this style of eating and thought it would translate well into a party format. It works in every season and for any reason. One of my favorite times of year for A Night in Venice party is the holidays. The water, lights and buffet-style service suit holiday entertaining perfectly, without pinning you down on Christmas, Hanukkah or any other religious observance.

The first time we tried out this party plan, I hosted it in my home. Everyone enjoyed tasting the Venetian-style food and wine, and we partied well into the night. The following year, our friend used the party plan for a holiday party she was hosting for more than 100 people. Elizabeth and I helped her transform a pool table into a towering tablescape of water, candles and delicious desserts. Undoubtedly, an event to remember!

Ignite Your Spirit

A NIGHT IN VENICE

A NIGHT IN VENICE was carefully crafted to give you and your guests a true taste of Venetian food and traditions, as well as allowing you to share the special wines from the Veneto region. Enjoy the treasured tradition of Cicchetti and Ombra with your family, friends, and neighbors. Gather together with loved ones and friends from all backgrounds and faiths to share in the common wish for peace and harmony. Celebrate the radiant spirit of Venice and let the enchantment of this liquid city be a "clear and shining" example of the sparkling brilliance in all of us.

VIBE
√ Radiant
√ Cosmopolitan
√ Harmonious

Review Party Plan

THE PARTYBLUPRINTS A NIGHT IN VENICE is an evening party designed to transport your guests to a magical place full of festivity and life. Your Party Plan, a thoroughly coordinated "bluprint," details the concept, design, materials, and methods. We've put all the essential information and helpful tools at your fingertips. Simply follow your set of bluprints (Party Plan) and start building your party now.

SCALE 1½" - 1 FT.	SKETCH SHEET.
DRAWN BY:	
TRACED BY:	
CHECKED BY:	DATE

PARTYBLUPRINTS = ARCHITECT
YOU = BUILDER

This Party Plan is your set of "bluprints"
for building your party.
You are the "U" in Partybluprints.

Your set of bluprints contains the following:

SCOPE & CORE ELEMENTS (Concept & Foundation)

SPECS (Party Components)

FOOTPRINT (Layout, Detailed Specs, Flow & Tablescape)

ARCHITECT'S NOTES (Insider's Tips)

MATERIALS LIST (Shopping List)

CRITICAL PATH (Timeline/To-Do List)

Scope & Core Elements

CONCEPT & FOUNDATION

Light Up Your Night

WHO	Adults Only or Family
WHAT	Dinner Party/Buffet Style
WHERE	Your Home
WHEN	Evening
WHY	To Celebrate Life
HOW	Follow Bluprint

BRING THE SPIRIT OF VENICE INTO YOUR HOME and create a shining and serene space for your guests where you all can "enjoy life." Transform your home into a place where beauty and light glimmer around every corner (we'll show you how in the Footprint section). Inspired by a vibe that is radiant, cosmopolitan, and harmonious, you will build your party using these core elements: golden sparkling candlelight, water, and Venetian inspired cocktails, wine, and food.

Specs

PARTY COMPONENTS

WE BELIEVE the most effective and enjoyable approach to entertaining is to start with a plan that stimulates all five senses. There are six key party components in every PARTYBLUPRINTS PARTY PLAN:

Invitations　　　　Cocktails　　　　Food

Music　　　　Special Activities　　　　Favors

The Specs section details the materials and structural notes for each party component. Pay attention to all of the components of your party and make sure they enhance, and do not detract, from one another. Consider this party a symphony for the senses: vision, palate, aroma, acoustics, and feeling. If you achieve the right balance, your guests' senses will be satisfied, which results in relaxed, happy guests and the perfect party environment!

Invitations

In honor of the City of Water, "float" an invitation in a bottle to your guests.
Create your own invitations (use plastic bottles, not glass) or purchase a kit.
Pen a note to each guest, insert in bottle, cork, package, label, and send
it on its way. This unique invitation won't go unnoticed in your guests' mail.
It sets the perfect tone for your party as it recalls the long-ago means
of communication in the archipelago of islands that comprise Venice.

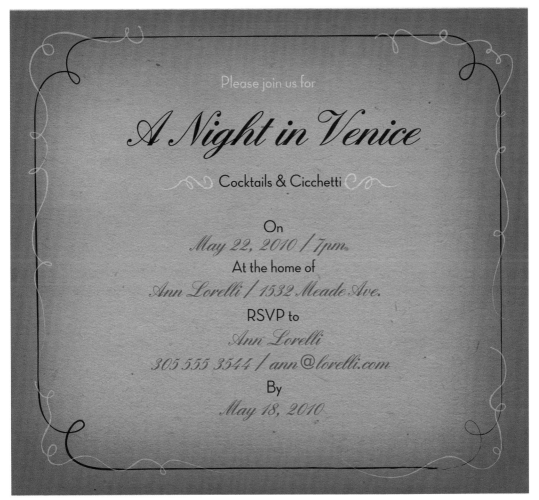

Please join us for

A Night in Venice

Cocktails & Cicchetti

On
May 22, 2010 / 7pm

At the home of
Ann Lorelli / 1532 Meade Ave.

RSVP to
Ann Lorelli
305 555 3544 / ann @lorelli.com

By
May 18, 2010

*Partybluprints Pick: Invitation in a Bottle has a variety of kits to choose from. Try the
aged or gold parchment paper tied with a gold ribbon in a plastic bottle.*
BUILDER'S NOTE: *Use your own personal flair to create your invitation. If desired, note dress
(formal, casual chic, etc.) on bottom of invitation.*

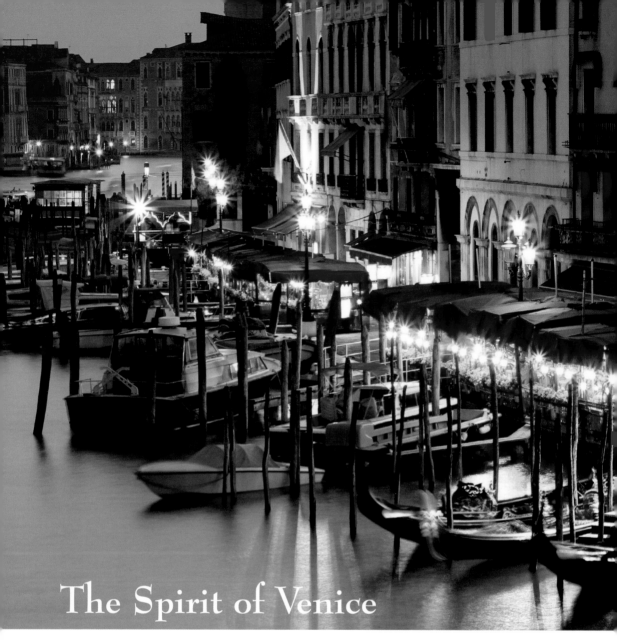

The Spirit of Venice

SOME REFER TO VENICE AS LA SERENISSIMA, "the most serene," others call it the most romantic place on earth, and still others cite it as "The City of Water." Regardless of the moniker, Venice is undeniably a unique and gracious city; she touches everyone and gives a "peace" of herself to all who embrace her. This enchanting land is surrounded by water, infused with sparkling brilliant light, and filled with glistening golden treasures. The beauty, majesty, and charm of Venice reflect more a spirit than a place.

A city is not alive without its people, and the one thing Venetians know how to do is enjoy life, as evidenced by their proclamation: "We work to live, not live to work." The locals love to socialize while "taking" a small glass of wine, Ombra, at the wine bar while enjoying Cicchetti, Venetian tapas-like snacks. Conviviality fills the air as conversation, food, and drink are shared. This is the perfect Venetian venue to socialize, laugh, and enjoy life.

Peace is a state of harmony. The magical land that would grow to become the Republic of Venice was founded upon a desire for this state. Seeking a peaceful way of life, the early inhabitants of Venice fled from the barbarians and escaped to the

marshland. With nothing more than a strong spirit, these refugees and their followers built a foundation for a unique and brilliant city.

From its dawn, Venice opened itself to the world. People of all nationalities and cultures set up shop side-by-side, bartering their goods and sharing their traditions. Trading from the streets and squares of Venice would soon grow to include transcontinental commerce. Venice thrived as a commercial crossroads for more than a thousand years, enjoying an illustrious era. Although this commercial success would wane, the influence of various and distant cultures would survive, interwoven into a rich and cosmopolitan tapestry that would forever be Venice.

The spirit of Venice is immortalized in the architecture and physical landscape. The flowing waterways and narrow cobblestone streets lead you through a city of mesmerizing beauty. The waterways are the arteries of this city and recall a time when they were the lifeblood of commerce. As you weave in and out of the canals and streets, every turn reveals another facet of the city's history. A story is forever emblazoned on every building and monument.

Now that you've invited
your guests,
it's time to plan your menu.
Here are our
Partybluprints Picks:

A Night in Venice

Menu

Cocktails

Tramezzini Trio
Paired with White Peach Bellini Cocktail

Cicchetti

Fried Olives
Italian Charcuterie and Cheese
Seafood and Arugula Salad
Rialto Baked Polenta
Meatballs
Rice Balls
Paired with the Wines of Veneto
Ombra Style

Dolce

Chocolate Cake
Venetian Ribbon Cookies
Italian Cheesecake
Assorted Biscotti
Tiramisu Cake
Paired with Sgroppino Dessert
Cocktail

Cocktails
(Serves 20)

WHITE PEACH BELLINI

Graciously greet your guests with the ultimate Venetian cocktail,
the Bellini, a delicious combination of Prosecco and white peach puree.
The effervescence of this signature cocktail immediately conveys
the spirit of the evening.

Materials
4 bottles Prosecco
20 oz. white peach puree

Structural Notes
❖ Thaw white peach puree.
❖ For each guest, pour one ounce of white peach puree into a champagne flute.
❖ Slowly add four ounces of Prosecco.
❖ Stir and serve.
❖ Display champagne flutes and materials on one end of Bacaro/Wine Bar.
Partybluprints Picks: White Peach Puree—The Perfect Puree of Napa Valley.
Prosecco—Adami Prosecco.

THE STORY BEHIND THE BELLINI

In 1948, the head bartender at Harry's Bar in Venice, Giuseppe Cipriani, combined his love for Italian white peaches with Italy's beloved sparkling wine, Prosecco. When he knew he had a winner, Cipriani named this cocktail the Bellini, after the Venetian painter, Giovanni Bellini. This Venetian cocktail is a classic.

Cocktails

TRAMEZZINI TRIO

Tramezzini are popular thin, crustless, triangular sandwiches served in bacari (wine bars). You will find these tempting treats stacked in glass cases, sometimes right at the store window. These tasty triangles became popular in Italy after World War II, when American servicemen introduced Italians to their version of white sandwich bread.

Partybluprints Picks for the Tramezzini Trio:

> *The Italian BLT: Tomato, Crisp Crumbled Pancetta, Red Leaf Lettuce, and Cream Cheese;*
> *The Adriatic Trade: Prosciutto and Red Pepper Hummus; and*
> *A Salute to the Red, White, and Green: Roasted Red Pepper, Fresh Mozzarella, and Pesto.*

Tramezzini Trio Materials

2 loaves of Pepperidge Farm Very Thin White Bread
1 lb. fresh mozzarella, room temperature and drained—sliced thin
1 (6 oz.) container pesto
1 jar roasted red peppers, drained and sliced thin
1 (8 oz.) container roasted red pepper hummus
½ lb. prosciutto, sliced thin
1 lb. pancetta, cooked very crisp and crumbled
1 head red leaf lettuce, washed and dried
3 large red tomatoes
1 (12 oz.) tub of whipped cream cheese

Structural Notes

❖ Tramezzini should be served thin and elegant, never overstuffed or sloppy. This is not a typical American sandwich. If you add too much filling, it will be difficult to eat. Remember to slice the ingredients for the Tramezzini thin.

❖ These are served as an appetizer—the perfect tantalizing taste for a hungry guest looking to enjoy a cocktail and socialize at the same time.

❖ For each Tramezzini, spread the binding agent (e.g., cream cheese, pesto, or red pepper hummus) over the entire slice of bread. Then, top each accordingly (see our recommendations above) with remaining ingredients and cover with second slice of bread.

- When Tramezzini are finished, wrap them in plastic wrap, and refrigerate for at least four hours to allow the flavors and ingredients to bind together.
- Remove the plastic wrap. Using a sharp knife, cut the crust off all four sides and slice each sandwich diagonally, creating two Tramezzini.
- Place each Tramezzini in a cocktail napkin, arrange on tray. This portion size allows your guests to eat it with one hand in about two bites.
- Let the Tramezzini come to room temperature, and keep covered with a damp paper towel until you are ready to serve.
- For a total of forty Tramezzini, make: ten Italian BLT (yields twenty Tramezzini); five Adriatic trade (yields ten), and five Salute the Red, White, and Green (yields ten).

BUILDER'S NOTE: *These recommendations allow for two Tramezzini per guest. If you think you have a heartier crowd, you can adjust the amount of materials and prepare additional Tramezzini.*

Cocktails

CICCHETTI (CHI-KET-TEE) AND OMBRA

Small snacks or appetizer size plates of food served in Cicchetti Bars in Venice along with Ombra, a small glass of wine

OMBRA

Ombra, a small glass of wine, is Cicchetti's companion. In Venice, bacari are small, stand-up wine bars that sell glasses of wine called Ombra, the Italian word for shade—this is where wine is stored in a city without cellars. Ombra is served in small glasses with Cicchetti. Veneto's winning whites and robust reds, offered as "Ombra," provide a tasting experience with Cicchetti.

Partybluprints Picks:
> Cesari "Nibai" Soave
> Montresor "La Colombaia" Pinot Grigio
> Cesari Amarone della Valpolicella
> Cesari "Mara" Ripasso
Check your local wine shop or online resources.

Materials
6 bottles Italian white wine
12 bottles Italian red wine

Structural Notes
❖ In the spirit of Cicchetti and Ombra, offer your guests white or red wine to pair with the Cicchetti.
❖ Offer non-alcoholic beverages such as Limonata (an Italian style lemon drink), plain water and sparkling water.

....

BUILDER'S NOTE: This is the perfect opportunity to take your "vintage" wine glasses (and dessert wine glasses, too) out to get some use. Your Ombra glasses should hold at least 4 oz. of wine. Also, if you have not established a relationship with a local wine proprietor, seek out some experts by visiting wine shops in your area. Wine experts can be an excellent resource and help you to explore your preferences.

EXPERT COMMENTARY

Kirk Sprenger, Wine Expert and Proprietor of The Chappaqua Wine & Spirit Company, Chappaqua, N.Y.

Comments from Kirk on Partybluprints Picks:

When one thinks of Veneto, pictures of the Adriatic Sea and incredible landscapes flood the mind. The region was named for the Venets, who first settled there in 1000 BC. These peaceful traders, who settled in the tranquil and picturesque region of Northern Italy, were looked upon very highly. The same can be said of many of the white wines from the area: serene.

One of the most well-known whites is Soave Classico. Though they lost their popularity back in the early 1990s, in part due to the mass production of some labels, they are making a strong comeback among oenophiles. Typical Soave is produced from the Garganega and Trebbiano grapes. Light, delicate flavors with almost a slight hint of floral in the bouquet are true characteristics. One of my favorites is Cesari's "Nibai" Soave Classico. It carries all the traits of what one would expect in the traditional style. Pair this with a sharp, hard cheese and some olives and it is a great match. The crisp acidity of the Soave helps to counterbalance the sharpness of the cheese and the salt of the olives.

Perhaps the most recognized grape of the region is Pinot Grigio. It accounts for the largest production of white wines in the area. I discovered Montresor's "La Colombaia" Pinot Grigio several years ago. It is definitely a house favorite. It has the essence of typical Pinot Grigio, with hints of nuts in the bouquet, yet has a very rounded feel on the palate not found in most Pinot Grigios. This will pair nicely with many seafood choices, such as shrimp, crabs, mussels, or scallops.

Before jumping into these white choices for your meal, I think it is always a good idea to cleanse your palate with a sparkling wine from the region known as Prosecco. It is a drink that can be enjoyed at almost any time. Prosecco is a crisp style of bubbly without the huge explosion of froth in the mouth that accompanies many Champagnes. Again, the peacefulness of the Venets. Adami Prosseco is one that I have found that is exceptionally good. It has a burst of flavor, a crisp texture, and finite bubbles.

The red wines of the region command a different respect. The wines of Valpolicella, named for a valley just north of the city of Verona, tend to show a bolder, more robust quality. The king of the region is Amarone della Valpolicella. Made from primarily Corvina grapes, this wine is prepared in a method like no other. The grapes are harvested in clusters and "racked" to be partially dried for anywhere between thirty and ninety days. This drying process helps to spike the sugar concentration and intensify the flavor. The grapes are then pressed, fermented, and aged for about twenty-four months. All of the sugars are transformed into alcohol yielding a final product of about 14 to 17 percent alcohol by volume. Cesari's Amarone della Valpolicella is bursting with ripe and spicy fruit with accents of dried figs. This beauty will certainly stand up to game, lamb or any heartier meat. For those looking for a tamer version, Valpolicella also produces a "Ripasso." The Valpolicella Classico begins its fermenting stage, then dried grapes from the Amarone wines are added to the mix to supplement the flavors and enrich the wine. This gives life, character, and longevity to what would be a simple table wine. Again, Cesari does this in one of my favorite Italian reds called "Mara" Ripasso. Its bold and luscious flavors seem to melt in your mouth.

Food

CICCHETTI
(Serves 20)

Venetians love their Cicchetti and Ombra. This time-honored tradition is a cherished part of the day: eating, drinking and socializing at the *bacaro* (the wine bars serving Cicchetti and Ombra), then spilling out into the streets of Venice and meandering over to the next *bacaro*. This favorite pastime is commonly referred to as the Venetian pub-crawl. The *bacaro* offer a variety of Cicchetti ranging from appetizer to "small plates" (tapas style) menu items. By the time you have "sampled" along the way, you have eaten a meal!

This Cicchetti buffet elegantly presents a twist on some Venetian favorites, adding up to one festive, delectable, and satisfying meal.

FRIED OLIVES

Fried olives are a gift from Venice. Olive lovers will go crazy for these little treasures. Your guests will not believe you made them yourself, and the best part is they are easy to prepare.

Materials
50 pitted green olives, drained and dried
1 cup flour
2 eggs, beaten
1 container Panko breadcrumbs (Japanese style)—white, not wheat
1 cup olive oil

Structural Notes
❖ Heat olive oil in frying pan (if you have a deep fat fryer, you can use that).
❖ Using three pie dishes (or containers with a flat bottom but rimmed edge), fill one dish with flour, another with beaten eggs, and the third with breadcrumbs.
❖ Dredge olives in flour, then cover in egg, and coat in breadcrumbs.
❖ Fry in oil, turning to fry all sides, until brown and crispy.
❖ Place on paper towel to absorb excess oil. Cool, cover, and set aside.
❖ Serve room temperature with Italian Charcuterie and Cheese plates.

Food

Italian Charcuterie and Cheese

Among our three Italian featured cheeses is Asiago, a treasured product from Veneto. Enjoy the interesting tastes and textures of these different cheeses with sopressata and dry sausage.

Partybluprints Picks:
> Italian Charcuterie—Dry Sausage and Sopressata, Murray's Cheese, N.Y., N.Y.
> Italian Cheeses—Asiago d'Allevo, igourmet
> Pecorino Foglie De Noce and La Tur, Murray's Cheese, N.Y., N.Y.

Materials

2 lbs. Asiago
2 lbs. Pecorino
2 (8 oz.) rounds of La Tur
4 (3.5 oz.) dry sausage or dry
   sausage totaling 1 lb.

2 (10 oz.) sopressata links
2 large French baguettes
4 boxes grissini
2 bags crostini

Structural Notes

❖ Line two clear glass platters with parchment paper to create your "plate." Arrange equal amounts of cheese, along with crostini (crackers), grissini (thin breadsticks), and thinly sliced baguettes on each plate. Each should serve ten guests.

❖ Cut the three cheese selections into individual portions. Do not cube the cheese; slicing it correctly yields more flavor. Your plates should be simple, yet elegant.

❖ Using a cheese knife, slice the Asiago and Pecorino cheese as you would a sliver of cake. Do not lob off the end. The artisan spent too much time crafting these cheeses for you to taste only a portion of them. When sliced correctly, you'll get the full taste of the cheese—from the inside out. Once you've cut the slivers, slice them in half horizontally for individual sized portions.

❖ Slice the La Tur into individual wedges, like a serving of cake. This fresh combination of goat, sheep, and cow's milk cheese is extremely soft and becomes more difficult to cut and arrange as it warms up. Leave it in the refrigerator until ready to cut and plate.

❖ Always serve cheese at room temperature. If you remove the cheese from the refrigerator one hour before serving, the true flavor of the cheese will emerge.

❖ Display the Italian Charcuterie and Cheese plates in different locations to encourage meandering just like in Venice.

SEAFOOD AND ARUGULA SALAD

This salad is our tribute to Venice's mainstay—seafood. The Venetians have always relied upon the "catch of the day" and are flexible in their menus. Since you will be serving a number of guests who may not appreciate the authentic Venetian seafood (cuttlefish, octopus), we feature shrimp and scallops. Although this recipe is less exotic, the combination of the succulent seafood, lemon, and peppery arugula is perfect.

Food

Seafood and Arugula Salad

Materials
2 lbs. salad shrimp
2 lbs. bay scallops
4 bags baby arugula rouquette, prewashed
1 cup high quality olive oil
1 cup fresh lemon juice (approx. 4 large lemons)
Sea salt to taste
Fresh cracked pepper to taste
1 lb. calamari (optional: use if available to you and if your guests would enjoy it)

Structural Notes

MARINADE/DRESSING
❖ Juice room temperature lemons.
❖ Whisk together lemon juice, olive oil, salt, and pepper.
❖ Set aside.

SEAFOOD AND ARUGULA SALAD
❖ Bring a large pot of water to a boil.
❖ Prepare an ice bath, a glass bowl filled with ice and water. Set aside.
❖ Carefully drop shrimp into boiling water. As soon as they turn pink
  (after approximately two minutes), remove from the pot and drop them
  in the ice bath to stop the cooking.
❖ When cool (approximately five minutes), drain, dry, and place them in large glass
  bowl (avoid using a metal bowl). Refrigerate.
❖ Add scallops to boiling water for one to two minutes. Remove and add to ice bath.
  When cool, drain, dry, and add to shrimp.
❖ If using calamari, repeat process.
❖ Once all the seafood is cooked, cooled, and combined, add half of the marinade
  and mix gently. Cover and refrigerate.
❖ When ready to serve, place arugula in a large shallow bowl/dish, add seafood
  and marinade, mix gently, and add dressing to taste. Be careful not to overdress;
  salad should be thoroughly coated with dressing, but not dripping.
❖ You may want to divide salad into two serving dishes, keeping one refrigerated
  and serving the other. Replenish as needed.

Food
(Yields two 13" x 9" trays)

Rialto Baked Polenta

We named this dish Rialto Baked Polenta because it is a meal that could be prepared from a shopping trip to the Rialto Market, a famous market in Venice. Venetians go to the market each day to buy the freshest ingredients. Such a trip may include polenta, sausage, onions, fresh plum tomatoes, and Fontina cheese. The purchases from this shopping trip combine to make a one-dish meal that is both satisfying and delicious— each bite holds a surprising combination of delectable tastes and textures.

Materials
2 (16 oz.) boxes cornmeal polenta
4 quarts (16 cups) water
8 tsp. salt
3 lbs. sweet Italian sausage (crumbled and cooked)
9 large plum tomatoes
Olive oil
Sea salt
1 lb. Fontina cheese, shredded
4 medium onions (sliced and caramelized)
Marinara sauce (optional)

Structural Notes
❖ Position one oven rack close to top of oven and preheat to 450 degrees.
❖ Wash and dry plum tomatoes. Cut tomatoes into ¼" slices. Arrange in a single layer on non-stick baking sheet, sprinkle lightly with olive oil and sea salt. Roast for ten minutes. Keep an eye on them and make sure they do not burn. When you see a brown edge forming on bottom of tomatoes, remove from oven. Cool and set aside.
❖ Grease two 13" x 9" baking dishes (if you are using a chafing dish, use 13" x 9" inserts) and set aside.
❖ Remove sausage from casings and crumble into large frying pan. Fry on medium heat until cooked thoroughly and crispy. Drain on paper towels and refrigerate.
❖ Heat two tablespoons of olive oil in pan and add sliced onions. Cook on medium

heat, stirring onions until caramelized (they should be translucent and golden brown) for approximately 30–40 minutes. If the onions start to burn or stick to pan, mix in a bit more olive oil. Cool and set aside.

❖ Pour 2 quarts (8 cups) of water into a six-quart pot, salt with 4 teaspoons salt. Bring to a boil. Turn heat down to low, and slowly stir in one box of cornmeal polenta. Vigorously stir with a whisk for 3–5 minutes until thick, smooth, and creamy. Turn off heat.

❖ Stir one-third of the cooked sausage into cornmeal polenta and pour into baking dish. Cover with a sheet of parchment paper and flatten top, then set aside. Repeat polenta preparation for second dish.

❖ Preheat oven to 350 degrees.

❖ Sprinkle the prepared casserole dishes with shredded Fontina cheese, caramelized onions, and the remaining sausage, and then top with roasted plum tomatoes. Neatly arrange tomatoes in a pattern of five rows by three columns. Use this as your guide when cutting the tray of polenta.

❖ Bake uncovered for thirty minutes or until bubbly and crispy on top. If not serving immediately, allow to cool slightly and refrigerate. When ready to serve, reheat at 350 degrees for twenty minutes, or until heated through. Precut into fifteen squares; one tomato should be at the center of each piece. Place in chafing dish to keep warm.

❖ Serve marinara sauce (homemade or your favorite brand) as an optional accompaniment.

Food

(Yields approximately 48 small meatballs)

MEATBALLS

Here's our twist on a traditional Cicchetti treat: meatballs. Inspired by our families' love of meatballs—they are a tradition on our Sunday dinner tables—we used Elizabeth's family recipe and tweaked it for our Cicchetti menu by simply reducing the size of the meatballs.

Materials
3 lbs. 80% or 85% lean ground beef
3 large eggs
2 ¼ cup seasoned breadcrumbs
3 cups marinara sauce
1 cup freshly grated Parmigiano Reggiano cheese

Structural Notes

- ❖ Preheat oven to 375 degrees. Line two baking sheets with aluminum foil, set aside.
- ❖ Add ground beef to oversized mixing bowl.
- ❖ Add remaining ingredients: eggs and breadcrumbs.
- ❖ Gently mix together with clean hands, just until all ingredients are mixed thoroughly.
- ❖ Spoon meatball mixture into palm of hand and gently form 1 ½" meatballs. While you don't want to "over roll" your meatballs, make sure they are solidly formed.
- ❖ Place meatballs on lined baking sheet 1" apart.
- ❖ Bake for fifteen to twenty minutes until cooked through.
- ❖ Remove from baking sheet and place on platter lined with paper towels to absorb excess oil.
- ❖ Allow to cool slightly and refrigerate.
- ❖ Just before serving, reheat in 375-degree oven for ten minutes until crispy and golden brown. Pour marinara sauce into bottom of chafing dish (just enough to liberally coat bottom), add meatballs, and you are ready to serve. Serve additional heated marinara sauce and freshly grated Parmigiano Reggiano cheese on the side.

Food

RICE BALLS

Risotto is a staple, in Venice and rice balls are a great way to pay tribute to this Venetian favorite. Rice balls are a treat in our families—a golden delicacy that is revered.

Partybluprints Picks: Our favorites, pictured here, are from Gino's Restaurant, Brooklyn, N.Y. If you are not local to the area, you can also order online from Landi's Pork Store in Brooklyn or try your local Italian restaurant, deli or market.

Materials
4 dozen small rice balls
Marinara sauce (optional)

Structural Notes
❖ Before guests arrive, heat rice in a 350-degree oven until warmed through. Then place in covered chafing dish to keep the food hot and moist. If you don't own any chafing dishes, borrow.
❖ Serve marinara sauce (homemade or your favorite brand) as an optional accompaniment.

DID YOU KNOW?
Venice has only 60,000 residents, yet welcomes between twelve to twenty million guests a year, making Venetians the consummate hosts.

Food

DOLCE—"Sweet"
Venetian Dessert Table

Dolce means "sweet" in Italian, and dessert is so sweet at this party. Our Venetian Dessert Table is inspired by the Italian tradition of the Viennese hour, an elaborate dessert hour, following a meal. The essence of the Viennese hour is the presentation of a multitude of desserts.

Prepare a Venetian Dessert Table laden with Italian dessert specialties and accented by golden floating candlelight. Your guests will be enamored by the beauty and richness of this display, which is the focal point of your party. You may choose to purchase all your sweets, do a combination of homemade and purchased, or prepare them all yourself.

ARCHITECT'S NOTE: We made a decision to purchase all our desserts for this party for a few reasons: (1) we found great online sources for the desserts that taste like you made them yourself; (2) we saved a significant amount of time ordering them as opposed to preparing ourselves; (3) we needed a great variety of desserts; and (4) the dessert items are a main element of your tablescape, so instead of purchasing flowers and other expensive items for the table, we invested in the desserts themselves.

Chocolate Cake

Every sweets table needs some chocolate.

Materials
1 chocolate cake

Structural Notes
❖ Purchase from your local bakery, supermarket or prepare your own.
❖ If you choose to purchase a chocolate cake, choose one that looks as good as it tastes.
❖ Display it on a cake pedestal and use it as the centerpiece for your Venetian Dessert Table (substitute it for our chocolate gondola in the picture).

Food

VENETIAN RIBBON COOKIES

These traditional Venetian cookies are a reminder of Venice's many different layers. Deep almond flavor, sophisticated apricot, and pure chocolate accents give these cookies a cosmopolitan air.
Partybluprints Pick: Two boxes of Venetian Ribbon Cookies from Veniero's Pasticceria & Caffe, N.Y., N.Y. You may also be able to purchase from your local bakery.

Materials
3 ½ dozen cookies

Structural Notes
❖ Arrange the colorful Venetian Ribbon cookies in a large-footed glass bowl.
❖ Display on Venetian Dessert Table.

ITALIAN CHEESECAKE

This traditional Italian dessert is rich with flavor and texture. It's airier and fluffier than New York style cheesecake.
Partybluprints Pick: Two 6" Italian Cheesecakes from Veniero's Pasticceria & Caffe, N.Y., N.Y. You may also be able to purchase from your local bakery.

Materials
2 small 6" Italian Style Cheesecakes

Structural Notes
❖ If you ordered it and froze it, take it out of the freezer the day before the party and let it thaw in the refrigerator.
❖ Keep refrigerated until ready to serve. The creamy inside and pastry crust combine for a smooth taste. Slice cheesecake into small slices and serve on a long, flat, rectangular glass platter/tray lined with parchment paper (parchment paper is a nicer alternative to wax paper).
❖ Display on Venetian Dessert Table.

BUILDER'S NOTE: Instead of two small cheesecakes, you can order one large. As always, you have the option to prepare your own.

Food

BISCOTTI

Biscotti are a cookie "baked twice" in the Italian traditional style. These Italian cookies are the perfect accompaniment to any dessert or for the guest who is looking for just a little something with their coffee.

Partybluprints Pick: We ordered two dozen assorted biscotti from Veniero's Pasticceria & Caffe, N.Y., N.Y. We marveled at the freshness, taste, and texture of these fabulous desserts.

Materials
2 lbs. assorted biscotti

Structural Notes
* Purchase and store in airtight container until ready to serve.
* Arrange the biscotti in a footed glass bowl or on a cake pedestal.
* Display on Venetian Dessert Table.

TIRAMISU CAKE

Venetians named this dessert Tiramisu because the words *"tira mi su"* literally mean "pick me up"—which is what the espresso and cocoa powder do! Sponge cake bathed in espresso and rum liqueur then layered with creamy Mascarpone cheese, dusted with cocoa, and sprinkled with chocolate pieces is a surprisingly creamy, dreamy dessert.

Materials
1 Tiramisu cake

Structural Notes
* Purchase from your local bakery, supermarket or prepare your own.
* Keep refrigerated until ready to serve.
* Slice into small slices and arrange on a parchment-lined flat, long glass rectangular tray/platter.
* Display on Venetian Dessert Table.

ARCHITECT'S NOTE: When we ordered online, we scheduled delivery for 2 days before the party to ensure delivery for the party. We kept the cheesecake and ribbon cookies frozen and left the biscotti airtight in the original wrapper.

Food

Sgroppino

In honor of the liquid city, take your guests by surprise with this "liquid dessert." This is another Venetian signature cocktail that will tickle your guests' fancy.

Materials
4 bottles chilled Prosecco
10 oz. chilled vodka
3 pints lemon sorbet

Structural Notes
❖ Use the same area you used at the beginning of the evening to prepare your Signature Cocktails. Simply replenish champagne flutes and Prosecco, trading out the peach puree for vodka and lemon sorbet.
❖ Pour 4 oz. ounces Prosecco into a champagne flute.
❖ Add a splash of vodka (approximately ½ oz.) and then add one scoop of sorbet.
❖ Serve immediately.

Coffee

Cap off the evening with a cup of coffee. The darkness of the coffee is a testament to the richness of the evening.

Materials
1 lb. coffee
Cream
Sugar

Structural Notes:
❖ Set up coffee maker before party begins. If you have or can borrow a coffee urn, it prepares double and triple the amount of a regular coffee maker.
❖ Serve with cream and sugar.
❖ As an added treat at your coffee station, include peppermint sticks as a refreshing addition or as a coffee stirrer. (The sticks are reminiscent of the poles at the gondola docks.)
❖ Brew before preparing Sgroppino Cocktails.

Special Touches

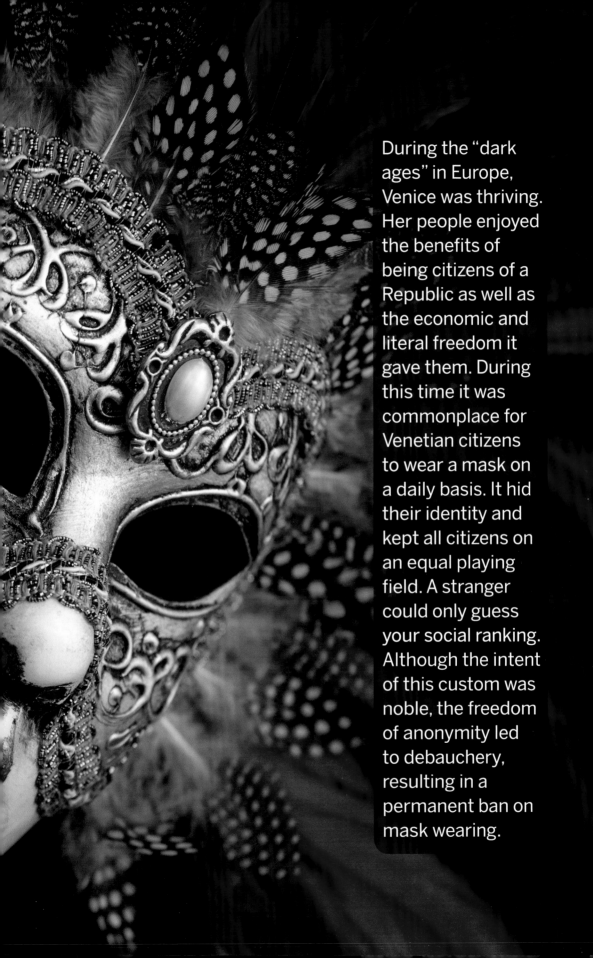

During the "dark ages" in Europe, Venice was thriving. Her people enjoyed the benefits of being citizens of a Republic as well as the economic and literal freedom it gave them. During this time it was commonplace for Venetian citizens to wear a mask on a daily basis. It hid their identity and kept all citizens on an equal playing field. A stranger could only guess your social ranking. Although the intent of this custom was noble, the freedom of anonymity led to debauchery, resulting in a permanent ban on mask wearing.

Music

Create a music mix or playlist for your A Night in Venice party. Feature artists such as Gruppo Venezia, Allegro Milano, and Sergio Lombardo, and treat your guests to a mix that blends traditional classical Venetian compositions with more modern Italian songs. It is sure to set the perfect mood for your guests.

Partybluprints Pick:
Partybluprints iTunes iMix, visit www.partybluprintsblog.com and click on "Book Links" category at the top of the homepage for details. Reminder: you can also find all the links for the Partybluprints Picks here.

Structural Notes

❖ Create a music mix specifically designed to coordinate with the vibe for this party.

❖ Set up sound system ahead of time and make sure it is fully functional.

❖ Have music playing when guests arrive.

❖ Dial into a good balance—not too loud, not too soft. Music should enhance, and not detract from, other elements.

❖ Whether you saved your music to a playlist or CD, continue to enjoy it. Every time you play it, you will rekindle the spirit of the evening.

Favors

Venice's signature emblem, the Winged Lion, represents Venice's motto, "Go forth in peace." This stately symbol is prominently displayed throughout the city as a proclamation of Venice's spirit. The sight of this majestic symbol in St. Mark's Cathedral is powerful.

Gift your guests a special favor and make a donation in their honor and in honor of the evening. As the evening comes to a close, present your guests with a keepsake commemorating the evening.

Partybluprints Pick: As a tribute to Venice and its spirit, we chose "Save Venice" as our designated charity for this party.

Structural Notes

❖ Purchase a bookmark kit (with plain white or antique white paper and tassels).

❖ Embellish the bookmarks with a stamp and gold ink or something that you feel represents the spirit of the evening, such as the word "Peace."

❖ On the back write: "A donation was made to [insert name of designated charity] in your honor. To learn more [insert charity's website address]. Go Forth In Peace."

❖ If you chose to make a donation to a designated charity and have trouble deciding on an amount, try this approach: determine how much you would have spent on favors, deduct the cost of your bookmark kit and supplies and donate the remaining amount in honor of all your guests.

❖ If you would rather gift your guests simply with a remembrance of the evening, substitute a personal note on the back of the bookmark including your name, the date and "A Night in Venice."

Special Activities

In honor of the Venetian mask and its original intentions, provide an activity to fuel conversation and encourage mingling.

Structural Notes

❖ Set out a large bowl at or near the Wine Bar/Bacaro.

❖ Provide small pieces of paper and pens.

❖ Have each guest write a little known fact about themselves on a piece of paper, fold it, and put it in the bowl.

❖ Once everyone has completed this, let each guest select a piece of paper from the bowl.

❖ They will need to match the paper with the author by the end of the evening.

❖ For a special touch, decorate the bowl by tying a Venetian mask around it.

Partybluprints Pick: Elizabeth's mom, Karen, brought a mask back from her trip to Venice. To purchase one, try an online resource.

Footprint

Layout & Detailed Specs

SET YOUR HOME AGLOW WITH VENETIAN GOLD and floating candles. Create a magical look and let your guests feel the festivity and spirit of Venice as soon as they step through your door. Venice looks like a floating city on water, its reflection captured on the Grand Canal. The table should reflect this image and have the same look and feel. You can easily create it by using large and small cylinders of differing heights filled with water and floating candles. These affordable glass cylinders can be reused for a myriad of decorating ideas. The idea of this tablescape is to create a dramatic look using the basic elements of water, gold, and candlelight. When you introduce the Dolce (sweets), the spirit and passion of Venice is sure to come alive on your table!

The following elements were hand-selected to build the vibe (radiant, cosmopolitan, and harmonious):

> **Water and Candlelight** | These unite to illuminate your table, providing the perfect backdrop for not only your food, but also for your guests—who doesn't look fabulous lit by candlelight?

> **Gold Candles** | These add sparkle and radiance to really set your tablescape (and home) aglow.

> **Food** | As in all Italian cities, the food is front and center, enhanced by a breathtaking setting.

These basic elements combine to create a mood that is reminiscent of dining along the Grand Canal.

Flow

CREATE A JOURNEY for your guests, which will lead them by glittering candlelight from room to room throughout the evening. Your Venetian Dessert Table is the star of your Footprint. Centrally locate your Venetian Dessert Table where guests can gaze at it all night long. Then choose a separate spot for your Cicchetti Bar and Bacaro/Wine Bar.

Structural Notes

> Walk around your home to determine the flow of your party. Scout out the site of your various stations.
> The location of your stations will determine the flow of your party. The goal is to provide areas where people can congregate and mingle. Guests should be able to flow effortlessly from one station to another and help themselves at the various stations:
> 1. **Venetian Dessert Table**
> 2. **Cicchetti Bar**
> 3. **Bacaro/Wine Bar**
> Determine if you need to rearrange any furniture or bring in additional seating/tables.
> It's always considerate to provide several small seating areas for your guests to relax and truly enjoy the vibe of the party. Create "vignettes" by grouping pillows, benches, stools, and small chairs around existing seating areas/cocktail table(s). Make sure your vignettes can seat at least three or four people.

Tablescape

THE VENETIAN DESSERT TABLE featuring an array of festive "sweets" illuminated by glowing golden and floating candlelight will be the shining star at your party. Create a tablescape inspired by the skyline of Venice by displaying desserts on cake stands and plates of varying heights. Be sure to showcase the Venetian Dessert Table in an area of your home where guests can congregate. Once they see it, it will be hard to keep them away!

PARTYBLUPRINTS

HOW TO BUILD A TABLESCAPE

1. Inventory Materials

2. Build Foundation

3. Add Structural Elements

4. Decorate

Tablescape Materials List

INCLUDED IN COMPREHENSIVE MATERIALS LIST

The Venetian Dessert Table featuring an array of festive "sweets" illuminated by glowing golden and floating candlelight will be the shining star at your party.

USE THESE MATERIALS TO CREATE YOUR TABLESCAPE:

> Gold tablecloth to fit your buffet table
> 1 dozen assorted glass cylinders
> Water
> Golden glass marbles
> 4 dozen floating candles
> Assorted gold pillar candles
> Serving pieces—assorted glass plates, footed bowls, cake pedestals, trays
> Dolce—your delectable desserts

ARCHITECT'S NOTE: Again, the food is the star at this table. There are no flowers—just food, candles, water, and gold!

Structural Notes

1. INVENTORY YOUR MATERIALS

Take your Materials List (included at end of plan), and go on a scavenger hunt in your home. Stick with a clear (glass/crystal) and gold palette. If you have any Murano glass, use it—we incorporated a Murano glass footed bowl and filled it with cookies. Select a "staging" area near your table. Deposit all items you have collected there. Then, "play" with the items and arrange them until you've built your tablescape. Store unused items.

2. BUILD FOUNDATION

Use a gold tablecloth as your foundation, and then begin to build your lagoon city on top.

3. ADD STRUCTURAL ELEMENTS

Glass cylinders | Arrange glass cylinders down center of your table. Make sure to be random and do not arrange symmetrically or group like heights together. Imagine the skyline of Venice as seen from the Grand Canal—some buildings are tall, some short, some in between.

Gold pillar candles | Arrange various size candles amidst the cylinders.
Water | Fill glass cylinders ½ to ¾ full of water, varying the water levels.
Gold accents | Add golden glass marbles to the glass cylinders. Optional: add other gold accents such as glittering balls and objects as an additional element of sparkle and dimension to the tablescape.
Floating candles | Add the floating candles to the water-filled glass cylinders.
Serving pieces | Select footed bowls, glass platters/trays, and cake pedestals for Dolce (dessert). Then arrange selected serving pieces throughout your tablescape so they highlight the multitude of desserts displayed. If you have a special serving piece or Venetian momento (Murano glass, gondola) use it as the centerpiece of your desserts.

4. DECORATE

Just before your guests arrive, add the Dolce (sweets) to the Venetian Dessert Table.

BUILDER'S NOTE: Murano glass is a beloved product from the Venetian island, Murano. Murano glass is produced in many forms ranging from glasses and serving pieces to jewelry.

LIGHTS OUT IS A MUST!

After you have lit all the candles, dim the lights or turn them off altogether. Everything and everyone should be illuminated by candlelight. Make sure you have your backup supply of votive candles handy in case you need to replace any as the night goes on. *BUILDER'S NOTE: Instructions for setting up your cocktails and food are in the Structural Notes sections of Cocktails and Food. Try to incorporate some gold and floating candlelight at every station.*

CICCHETTI BAR

Materials
Fried Olives
Italian Charcuterie and Cheese
Seafood and Arugula Salad
Rialto Baked Polenta
Meatballs
Rice Balls

Structural Notes

> Venetian Cicchetti Bars are similar to deli/sandwich shops in the U.S. The various Cicchetti dishes are lined up under glass. The patrons select different Cicchetti dishes to create a tasting plate. Customers eat at the Cicchetti Bar standing up while enjoying a small glass of wine, Ombra, with their meal.

> You can create your Cicchetti Bar on a table or island in the kitchen. Make sure there is ample room for your guests to peruse the Cicchetti and make their selections. If using a table, cover it with a gold tablecloth.

> In addition, if space permits, incorporate some of the same elements from the main tablescape. Just be careful where you put the candles—you do not want guests to get burned reaching to serve themselves.

> At the Cicchetti Bar, display glass plates (you can purchase inexpensive glass plates at your local kitchen supply store and use them as a supplement to your kitchen essentials when entertaining a crowd).

> Roll utensils in white or gold linen napkins and tie with gold or white tassel. This is both an elegant and handy presentation.

> Arrange various chafing and serving dishes so guests can easily help themselves.

> Follow instructions in Food Section for prepping food for your Cicchetti Bar just before guests arrive.

BACARO/WINE BAR

Materials
(See Signature Cocktail, Ombra, and Dessert Cocktail section for Materials and Structural Notes)

Structural Notes

> To create your Bacaro/Wine Bar, continue the motif of water, gold, and candles on a much smaller scale, displaying a small glass cylinder with floating candles. The use of a gold candle is dependent on available space.

> You will need ample room, perhaps even an extra table, to keep all the glasses handy.

> With twenty guests, you will need forty flutes (if you only have twenty flutes, you will have to have someone wash them after the Signature Cocktails are finished) and at least twenty Ombra glasses!

> Display wine glasses and wine on one end of your Bacaro (the other end can be used for Signature Cocktail/Dessert Cocktail).

> Optional: use shorter wine glasses (around 4" tall) to convey the spirit of Ombra (you can use an assortment of small glasses as some restaurants do or use a standard set).

BUILDER'S NOTE: Candles always create great ambiance. If you have available space in your entryway, powder room, and/or other rooms where guests will gather, display a candle. Votives are always a good option in heavily trafficked areas where there is a lot of movement or activity.

Architect's Notes

INSIDER'S TIPS

1 **You will need between sixty to eighty glasses for twenty guests**, so make a provision for the dirty glasses. Consider renting glasses for the party. Many companies drop off and pick up dirty!

2 **Optional: hire a bartender/server** for the evening; ask friends, neighbors and local restaurants/bars for recommendations. Walk them through how you would like the Bellini and Sgroppino prepared and served. Educate them on the wine selections so they can answer questions for your guests.

3 **If you choose to hire a server**, you can have him/her wash the flutes after the initial cocktail and restock them at the bar for the Sgroppino.

4 **Set up the Bacaro/Wine Bar** with chilled Prosecco and the featured wines. Open the reds an hour before serving to let them breathe and make sure not to serve the white too cold.

5 **Wine charms** are a great way to help guests keep track of their glasses. This party requires a lot of glasses to begin with so this is a great way to avoid the unnecessary use of additional glassware.

6 **Heat the Rice Balls, Polenta, and Meatballs thoroughly** in the oven. Chafing dishes are only meant to keep food warm, not to heat food. Buy extra Sternos as backup.

7 **Set out two sets** of serving utensils on each side of the chafing dishes, so guests can then help themselves from either side.

8 **Use a gas lighter** with extender handle to light all your candles—it gets the job done quicker than a book of matches.

9 **Have plenty of backup floating candles** and make sure to buy scentless. Replace as needed during the party. You want to keep the ambience you created going until the last guest leaves.

10 **Pre-slicing the cakes** and arranging them on a platters allows guests to easily help themselves. No waiting for the first person to cut into a cake at the party.

11 **Optional: Borrow or purchase a coffee urn.** Some serve up to forty cups. Set up a coffee station with urn, cream, sugar, cups, spoons, etc., before the party. One hour into the party, flip the switch, and the coffee will brew in half an hour.

12 **Remember the "U" in Partybluprints** and add your special touches. Whether it is through your decorating, introducing your guests to your favorite charity, or personalizing a favor for your guests with a "goodnight note," bring your "builder's inspiration" to your party.

Materials List

USE THE INCLUDED MATERIALS LIST as your inventory and shopping list all in one. Simply make a copy and check off items you have before doing any shopping. Then, as you shop, continue to inventory items until all materials are "in-house."

Be efficient and keep an updated copy of your list with you whenever you go shopping and update it in real time. This avoids over purchasing and last minute impulse shopping (we like to call it "panic purchasing"), resulting in unnecessary stress and expenditures.

Critical Path

FOLLOW THE INCLUDED CRITICAL PATH to manage your time and tasks so you are not overwhelmed or unprepared for your guests. This guide combines your to-do list and timeline for efficient and effective preparation and execution. We've removed the guesswork and streamlined the process. If you stick to the Party Plan, you can prepare everything ahead of time and be a guest at your own party. What a sweet reward for a job well done!

PARTYBLUPRINTS A NIGHT IN VENICE
MATERIALS LIST
SHOPPING LIST FOR 20

- [ ] 8 bottles Prosecco (for Bellini and Sgroppino)
- [ ] 6 bottles Italian white wine (see recommendations)
- [ ] 12 bottles Italian red wine (see recommendations)
- [ ] 1 (20 oz.) container Perfect Puree White Peach Puree
- [ ] 1 (750 ml) bottle vodka
- [ ] 6 large bottles Italian Sparkling Water (Pana)
- [ ] 2 dozen bottles Limonata
- [ ] 2 loaves Pepperidge Farm Very Thin White Bread
- [ ] 1 lb. fresh mozzarella
- [ ] 1 (6 oz.) container pesto
- [ ] 1 jar roasted red peppers, drained
- [ ] 1 (8 oz.) container roasted red pepper hummus
- [ ] ½ lb. prosciutto
- [ ] 1 lb. pancetta
- [ ] 1 head red leaf lettuce
- [ ] 3 large red tomatoes
- [ ] 1 (12 oz.) tub of whipped cream cheese
- [ ] 50 pitted green olives
- [ ] 1 cup flour
- [ ] 5 large eggs
- [ ] 1 container Panko breadcrumbs (white not wheat)
- [ ] 1 bottle olive oil (for frying and general cooking)
- [ ] 1 cup high quality olive oil (marinade/dressing)

- [ ] coarse sea salt, table salt, and fresh cracked pepper
- [ ] 2 lbs. Asiago cheese
- [ ] 2 lbs. Pecorino cheese
- [ ] 2 (8 oz.) rounds of La Tur cheese
- [ ] 2 (10 oz.) soppressata links
- [ ] 1 lb. dry sausage
- [ ] 2 large French baguettes
- [ ] 2 bags crostini
- [ ] 4 boxes grissini
- [ ] 2 lbs. salad shrimp, cooked
- [ ] 2 lbs. bay scallops, cooked
- [ ] 1 lb. calamari (optional)
- [ ] 4 bags baby arugula rouquette, prewashed
- [ ] 1 cup fresh lemon juice (approx. 4 large lemons)
- [ ] 2 (16 oz.) boxes cornmeal polenta
- [ ] 9 large plum tomatoes
- [ ] 3 lbs. sweet Italian sausage
- [ ] 4 medium onions
- [ ] 1 lb. Fontina cheese, shredded
- [ ] 3 lbs. 80% or 85% lean ground beef
- [ ] 2 ¼ cup seasoned breadcrumbs
- [ ] 8 cups marinara sauce (purchase or prepare your own)
- [ ] 1 container fresh grated Parmigiano Reggiano cheese
- [ ] 4 dozen small rice balls
- [ ] 3 pints lemon sorbet
- [ ] 1 chocolate cake

PARTYBLUPRINTS A NIGHT IN VENICE
MATERIALS LIST
SHOPPING LIST FOR 20

- ☐ 1 Tiramisu cake
- ☐ 3 ½ dozen Venetian ribbon cookies
- ☐ 2 lbs. assorted biscotti
- ☐ 2 small 6" Italian Style Cheesecakes or 1 large
- ☐ 20 gold/white napkins
- ☐ cocktail napkins (for Tramezzini and cocktails)
- ☐ Champagne flutes
- ☐ wine glasses
- ☐ clear glass dinner plates
- ☐ dessert plates
- ☐ utensils
- ☐ coffee
- ☐ cream and sugar
- ☐ peppermint sticks (optional)
- ☐ coffee cups

- ☐ coffee urn
- ☐ gold tablecloth (if covering the Cicchetti Bar you'll need two)
- ☐ 1 dozen assorted glass cylinders
- ☐ assorted gold pillar candles
- ☐ 4 dozen floating candles
- ☐ golden glass marbles
- ☐ serving pieces (assorted glass plates, footed bowls, cake pedestals, trays)
- ☐ 20 bookmarks, stamp and gold ink (favor)
- ☐ 40 tassels for both favor and accent to dinner napkins
- ☐ Venetian mask (optional)
- ☐ gas lighter with extender handle
- ☐ Sternos
- ☐ chafing dishes

NOTES

....
....
....
....
....
....
....
....

PARTYBLUPRINTS A NIGHT IN VENICE
CRITICAL PATH
TIMELINE/TO-DO LIST

Requires Immediate Attention (at least three weeks in advance)

☐ Choose the date for your Partybluprints A Night in Venice party.

☐ Create a guest list; consider your audience. Do you want to mix it up a little and make some introductions or invite a close circle of friends?

☐ Order or create your invitations, prepare them, and mail.

☐ Determine which items you have in stock (accessories, tableware, serving pieces, tools).

☐ Order any online items.

Two Weeks before the Party

☐ Order wine and Prosecco.

☐ Order the food and dessert; select your preferred delivery dates.

☐ Buy non-perishable items. (See Materials List.)

☐ Contact rental company if you are renting glasses and/or dishes.

☐ Optional: Hire a bartender and/or server.

☐ Purchase and make the bookmark favors.

The Week before the Party

☐ Inventory items for the party and purchase any items still needed.

☐ Walk around the inside of your home to determine the flow of your party.

Scout out the site of your various stations. The location of your stations will determine the flow of your party. Determine if you need to rearrange any furniture or need additional tables/chairs, etc.

☐ Test your sound system and settle on a playlist. Burn the list to CDs or store in your iPod or other similar device.

☐ Make a donation to your designated charity in honor of your guests.

One to Two Days before the Party

☐ Shop for any last minute items, e.g., fresh produce, seafood, cheese, meat, Tramezzini ingredients, and bread.

☐ Roll individual utensils in cloth napkins and tie with a tassel. Arrange on a tray.

☐ Print your menu and display in a pretty gold frame (this looks great at the Bacaro/Wine Bar).

One Day before the Party

☐ Prepare the Rialto Baked Polenta, cover, and refrigerate.

☐ Prepare meatballs and refrigerate.

☐ Prepare the Venetian Dessert Table with tablecloth, arrange pillar candles and glass cylinders. Cover bottom of cylinders with glass marbles; you can fill with water or wait until tomorrow. Set out the serving pieces and utensils for the desserts.

- ☐ Prepare Bacaro/Wine Bar station.
- ☐ Arrange glassware; make sure glasses are dust and spot free.
- ☐ Prepare Cicchetti Bar and arrange chafing dishes (make sure you have Sternos) and serving utensils (with the exception of the food).
- ☐ Put frozen dishes/desserts in refrigerator to thaw overnight.
- ☐ Take some time to choose an outfit in which you look and feel fantastic!

Morning of the Party

- ☐ Start the day off on a good note; it's the day of your party!
- ☐ Designate a time to get yourself ready and stick to it.
- ☐ Have a cup of coffee or whatever gets you going and start the final preparations for your party!
- ☐ Chill the Prosecco and white wine.
- ☐ Prepare fried olives and store in an airtight container until ready to serve.
- ☐ Prepare the Tramezzini according to recipe and refrigerate.
- ☐ Prepare seafood and marinade/ dressing and refrigerate—do not toss with arugula until ready to serve.

Four Hours before the Party

- ☐ Prepare Italian Charcuterie and Cheese plates. Cover and refrigerate.
- ☐ Set up coffee station.

Two Hours before the Party

- ☐ Take Rialto Baked Polenta out of refrigerator to bring to room temperature.

- ☐ Remember the "U" in Partybluprints and add your special touches (such as adding candlelight leading up to the front door and throughout your home).
- ☐ You followed the Partybluprints Party Plan and physically prepared the party, now it's time to prepare you. Shower and dress in something that makes you feel great. Let the excitement of your party envelop you.

One Hour before the Party

- ☐ Cut and arrange Tramezzini; cover with damp paper towel. You can leave this out of refrigerator.
- ☐ Fill chafing dishes with boiling water, light the Sternos.
- ☐ Heat polenta thoroughly and move to chafing dish.
- ☐ Reheat the meatballs until crispy and golden brown, place in chafing dish.
- ☐ Reheat the rice balls just until heated through (don't overheat) and move to chafing dish.
- ☐ Do a final walk through of all your stations.
- ☐ Open six bottles of red wine to allow them adequate time to breathe.

Thirty Minutes before the Party

- ☐ Put out Italian Charcuterie and Cheese platters and Fried Olives.
- ☐ Mix Seafood and Arugula Salad and display with Cicchetti.
- ☐ Display Dolce/"sweets" on Venetian Dessert Table.

Fifteen Minutes before the Party

☐ Start the music.

☐ Light the candles with an extended lighter.

☐ Take a walk around, admire your work, and feel the vibe.

☐ Pour yourself a cocktail and toast yourself for a job well done.

☐ Remove damp paper towel covering Tramezzini and serve.

Upon Guests' Arrival

☐ Trade them their coat for a Bellini Cocktail.

☐ Invite them to enjoy the Tramezzini; you can serve them as a passed hors d'oeuvres or set the tray out at the Bacaro/Wine Bar.

Thirty Minutes to One Hour into the Party

☐ Flip the switch on the coffee and replenish Seafood and Arugula Salad.

☐ Make sure everyone has a drink and invite your guests to enjoy the Bacaro/Wine Bar, Cicchetti Bar, and Venetian Dessert Table in whatever order they choose.

Two Hours into the Party

☐ Offer Sgroppino and coffee. Cheers!

NOTES

....

....

....

....

....

....

....

....

....

....

BEHIND THE BLUPRINT
—OUR PARTY NOTES

OUR LOVE OF WINE HAS LED US TO PAIR IT WITH SOME UNEXPECTED FOODS. Chocolate was one of them—once we tried it, we loved it. One late night, we spontaneously got together with our husbands at Dawn's house. She pulled together a plate of some dark chocolate candy and broke out a bottle of Cabernet (one of our usual "house drinks"). We started sipping our wine and then nibbled a piece of dark chocolate—oh yes, perfect pairing. The dark richness of this seductive combination had such a captivating quality, we decided to design a cocktail and dessert party around this dynamic duo. The vibe for this party had to be unmistakable—candlelight only.

Inspired and on a mission, we set out to find the best dark chocolate in New York City and our local area. We spent six months tasting dark chocolates of differing percentages of cacao, origins, and varietals and in all its glorious forms. With some help from our Resident Wine Expert, Kirk, we narrowed down the Cabernets (we wanted to stay at a reasonable price point), taste tested a few with the dark chocolate, and knew when we found just the right one. We were so excited to design, develop, and host a party. With chocolate, cabernet, and candlelight as the core elements and the vibe clear, the other party elements fell right into place.

Dawn and I co-hosted a Chocolate Soiree at her home. Not only did we have a memorable time with our friends, they had a great time as well, which is the biggest compliment. Dawn even received calls from the men at the party thanking us for such an outstanding evening. The buzz before and after the party was strong—excitement surrounding a party is always good.

The tables were turned on us when a friend followed the Party Plan, hosted a Chocolate Soiree in her home, and invited us as guests. She put her own unique touches on the party—it was fabulous! We love, love, love this party whether we host or are invited guests.

Indulge Your Desires

PARTYBLUPRINTS

CHOCOLATE SOIREE

DARK CHOCOLATE IS ONE OF THE MOST COVETED AND PERFECT FOODS ON EARTH.
Research even shows that it is good for your heart and brain. After hosting this soiree, you and your guests will testify that chocolate in this ultimate setting ignites not only the heart and brain, but arouses all the senses. This may prove to be the most stimulating party you'll ever host.

VIBE
√ Sensual
√ Self-Indulgent
√ Sophisticated

Review Party Plan

YOUR SET OF BLUPRINTS

THE PARTYBLUPRINTS CHOCOLATE SOIREE is an evening party designed to indulge your guests' appetites in many ways. The Soiree results in an extraordinary experience for the guests and the host. Your Party Plan, a thoroughly coordinated "bluprint," details the concept, design, materials, and methods. We've put all the essential information and helpful tools at your fingertips. Simply follow your set of bluprints (Party Plan) and start building your party now.

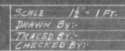

SCALE 1½" · 1 FT.
DRAWN BY :-
TRACED BY :-
CHECKED BY :-

SKETCH SHEET.

DATE

PARTYBLUPRINTS = ARCHITECT
YOU = BUILDER

This Party Plan is your set of "bluprints"
for building your party.
You are the "U" in Partybluprints.

Your set of bluprints contains the following:

SCOPE & CORE ELEMENTS (Concept & Foundation)

SPECS (Party Components)

FOOTPRINT (Layout, Detailed Specs, Flow & Tablescape)

ARCHITECT'S NOTES (Insider's Tips)

MATERIALS LIST (Shopping List)

CRITICAL PATH (Timeline/To-Do List)

Scope & Core Elements
CONCEPT & FOUNDATION

WHETHER YOUR HOME IS EXTRAVAGANT or modest, you can build a Hot Spot (we'll show you how in the "Footprint" section). A Hot Spot sparks a vibe that is sensual, self-indulgent, and sophisticated. The Hot Spot you create is the ultimate setting to showcase your soiree's three core elements: Cabernet, chocolate, and candlelight. You'll build upon this foundation according to the specs, then light the candles, dim the lights, and put on some soulful music. Let the soiree begin!

Create A Hot Spot

WHO	Strictly Adults
WHAT	Cocktails & Desserts
WHERE	Your Home
WHEN	Evening
WHY	To Have Fun
HOW	Follow Bluprint

Specs

PARTY COMPONENTS

WE BELIEVE the most effective and enjoyable approach to entertaining is to start with a plan that stimulates all five senses. There are six key party components in every PARTYBLUPRINTS PARTY PLAN:

Invitations

Cocktails

Food

Music

Special Activities

Favors

The Specs section details the materials and structural notes for each party component. Pay attention to all of the components of your party and make sure they enhance, and do not detract, from one another. Consider this party a symphony for the senses: vision, palate, aroma, acoustics, and feeling. If you achieve the right balance, your guests' senses will be satisfied, which results in relaxed, happy guests and the perfect party environment!

Invitations

Your invitation should reflect the vibe of your party.
Use a simple yet sophisticated style, and give your guests
a taste of things to come. Try something like this:

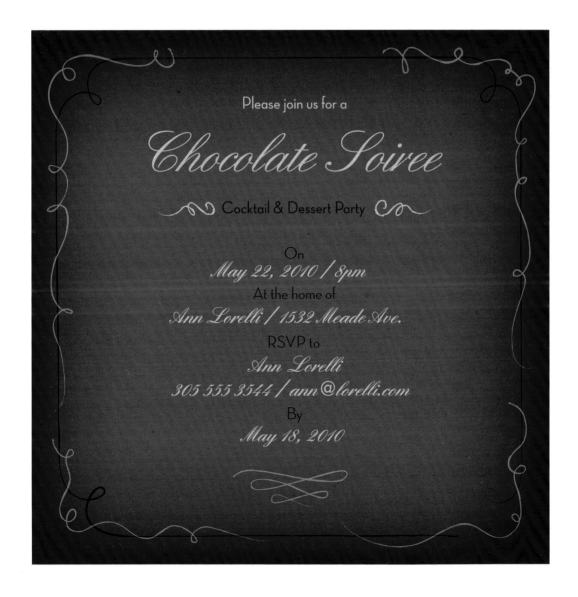

Please join us for a

Chocolate Soiree

Cocktail & Dessert Party

On
May 22, 2010 / 8pm
At the home of
Ann Lorelli / 1532 Meade Ave.
RSVP to
Ann Lorelli
305 555 3544 / ann @lorelli.com
By
May 18, 2010

Now that you've invited
your guests,
it's time to plan your menu.
Here are our
Partybluprints Picks:

Chocolate Soiree

Menu

Cocktails

Prosecco
Cabernet Sauvignon

Desserts

Chocolate Cake
Pots de la Crème
Artisanal Chocolates
Chocolate Almond Bark
Intermezzo Berries
Chocolate Tasting Bar
Liquid Chocolate Shots

Cocktails

(Serves 20)

PROSECCO SIGNATURE COCKTAIL

Welcome your guests with a glass of Prosecco (Italian sparkling wine). A glass of bubbly will magically relax your guests, while piquing their anticipation for the evening ahead. *Partybluprints Pick: Adami Prosecco for a clean, crisp taste that does not compete with the sweetness of the chocolate. Check your local wine shop or online resources for availability.*

Materials
4 (750 ml) bottles Prosecco

Structural Notes
❖ Set up a "welcome to the evening" station near the inside entrance of your home. Offer glasses of Prosecco and sparkling water, both served in champagne flutes.
❖ One 750 ml bottle of Prosecco serves six guests—it's meant only to kick off the evening. If you anticipate that some guests may choose to continue drinking Prosecco, stock up on a few more bottles. The majority of guests will choose to switch over to wine after the signature cocktail.
❖ **Optional:** For a splash of color and style, add a berry or two to the cocktails.

CABERNET SAUVIGNON WINE

Choose a Cabernet that complements the dark chocolate, and you will surprise your guests with this pairing that is sure to stimulate the senses. *Partybluprints Pick: Hess Select Cabernet Sauvignon; it pairs wonderfully with the chocolate. Check your local wine shop or online resources.*

Materials
15 (750 ml) bottles Cabernet Sauvignon

Structural Notes
❖ General rule of thumb: two to three glasses of wine per guest (there are four glasses to a bottle).
❖ Set up a wine bar with plenty of Cabernet, wine glasses, a wine bottle opener, salted mixed nuts, and pretzel crisps.
❖ Open a few bottles at a time and let them breathe before pouring.
❖ If you have a "co-host," have him/her clear the champagne flutes. Otherwise, enlist a helping hand.
❖ As the glasses are being cleared, follow behind with a tray of Cabernet, sparkling water, and still water. This provides you, as host, an opportunity to check in personally with guests.

EXPERT COMMENTARY

Kirk Sprenger, Wine Expert and Proprietor
of The Chappaqua Wine & Spirit Company,
Chappaqua, N.Y.

*Comments from Kirk on Partybluprints
Picks: Prosecco and Cabernet Sauvignon
Pairing with Dark Chocolate*

As guests enter your home for any type of occasion,
whether it is for a dinner party, the holidays, or an
intimate social gathering, a perfect welcome is a
glass of Prosecco. This is the delicate sparkling wine
from Italy that goes with "hello." It is light, crisp, and
unobtrusive. One of my favorites is Adami Prosecco.
It is flavorful and crisp, yet it seems to disappear
with just a soft lingering finish.

As guests settle in for an evening of decadence
and indulgence, the atmosphere needs to be sensual and sophisticated. Nothing sets the tone for a
sensual and sophisticated evening more than candlelight, intimate friends, and deep dark chocolate. And
nothing matches the sophistication of deep dark
chocolate more than a deep rich Cabernet Sauvignon. While most of us think of a hearty red wine ac-
companying a beef roast or leg of lamb, many others
are enjoying these same reds either on their own or
with smaller tidbits. Wine need not always be paired
with a meal or with what is normally expected. The
essences of dark chocolate are bountiful enough to
stand up to a deep red wine. For this, a perfect choice
is Hess Select from Napa Valley. While boasting ripe
flavors of plum and black cherry, it also surprisingly
shows hints of chocolate. What is better than chocolate with chocolate? The texture, as well, is smooth
and velvety with soft tannins, complementing the
silkiness of creamy dark chocolate.

*BUILDER'S NOTE: If you have not established a relationship
with a local wine proprietor, seek out some experts by
visiting wine shops in your area. Wine experts can be an
excellent resource and help you to explore your preferences.*

Cocktails

WATER/NON-ALCOHOLIC BEVERAGES

Offer citrus-infused water in addition to several non-alcoholic beverages. Chocolate can make you thirsty, and water is the perfect thirst quencher and palate cleanser.

Materials
3 (1 liter) bottles sparkling water
3 (2 liter) bottles soda (Diet Coke, Sprite, ginger ale)
3 oranges
3 limes
3 lemons

Structural Notes

❖ Set up a Water/Non-Alcoholic Beverage Bar near the Wine Bar. Be sure the water bar is located in a prominent area.

❖ Collect a few glass pitchers and fill them with ice and water. Slice up some citrus fruits (oranges, lemons, and limes) and add to the pitchers. You can mix the fruits or keep them separate.

❖ Offer other non-alcoholic beverage options besides water, such as sparkling water and soda.

❖ Serve ice in an ice bucket.

❖ Make sure to replenish the water bar as necessary.

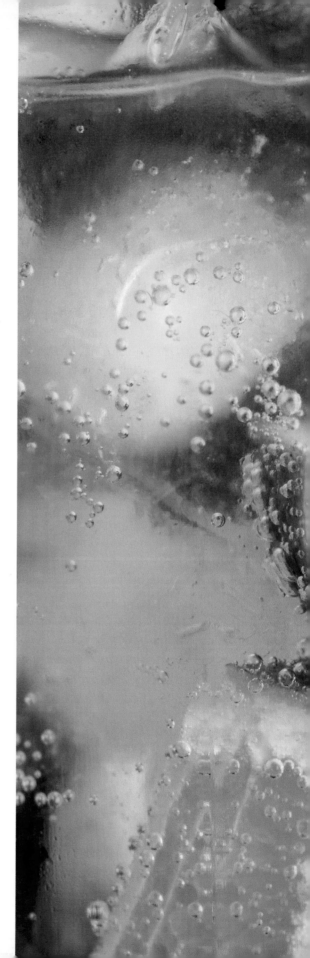

PARTYBLUPRINTS RULE OF GOOD MEASURE

"Always offer non-alcoholic beverages at your bar and table."

1. Be considerate of your guests—don't assume all your guests drink alcohol.

2. Offer a festive non-alcoholic alternative to your signature cocktail.

3. Support responsible drinking.

Food

CHOCOLATE—*In all its sinful forms*
(Serves 20)

CHOCOLATE CAKE

Seek out a fabulous looking and tasting chocolate cake at a local bakery or market. Choose something that is decadent!
Partybluprints Pick: Our favorite local bakery—CocoLuxe Fine Pastries, Peapack, N.J.

Materials
One large chocolate cake (you will be cutting smaller than usual pieces of cake for everyone to sample, so the cake does not need to serve 20).

Structural Notes
❖ Order the cake in advance for pick up the day before your party or morning of your party. Keep refrigerated until ready to serve.
❖ Display the cake on a cake pedestal, using it as a visual anchor on one end of your Dessert Buffet Table.
❖ Do not mar its beautiful presentation before guests arrive. Wait until guests begin the dessert buffet to cut slivers of cake. The pieces should be small. With the decadence of the evening, a little taste of everything is more than enough.
❖ If you prefer to make your cake, rely on a tried and true recipe.

....

DID YOU KNOW?
Throughout the ages, chocolate has represented a great many things to different people. The Mayans are the first on record to have enjoyed chocolate. Almost 2,000 years ago, the Mayans made a liquid drink from crushed cacao beans, called Xocoatl. This "liquid chocolate" was reserved for royalty and enjoyed at ceremonial events. During the rule of the Aztecs, Emperor Montezuma drank his liquid chocolate in goblets before entering his harem, propagating the popular belief that chocolate is an aphrodisiac.

Food

Pots de la Crème
Our twist on a traditional dessert

These petite pots filled with luscious dark chocolate and topped with fresh whipped cream and dark chocolate shavings are sure to pique the interest of all present. These easy-to-prepare spoonfuls of heaven are the perfect size to satisfy your guests' cravings.
Partybluprints Pick: Jacques Torres Classic Hot Chocolate mix, Jacques Torres Chocolate Haven, New York, N.Y.

Materials
1 (18 oz.) container Jacques Torres Classic Hot Chocolate mix
  (if you substitute a different brand, make a comparable substitution
  with comparable ingredients)
2 ½ cups 2% milk
Fresh whipped cream (recipe on pg. 198)
1 dark chocolate bar

Structural Notes:
❖ Measure one cup of milk for every one cup of Jacques Torres Classic Hot Chocolate mix. Pour milk into a saucepan and heat to just before a boil. Reduce heat and slowly add in chocolate while whisking vigorously until chocolate is dissolved (approximately one minute). Fill 20 small mugs/cups with chocolate mixture (¹/₂ to ³/₄ of the way full), cover with plastic wrap, and refrigerate at least four hours to set. The chocolate will magically transform from liquid to solid.
❖ You can prepare up to two days in advance.
❖ Just before serving, top Pots de la Crème with a dollop of fresh whipped cream, and sprinkle top with chocolate shavings.
❖ To create chocolate shavings, use a vegetable peeler and peel the long edge of a dark chocolate bar just as you would a carrot or use a grater.
❖ Display on your Dessert Buffet Table.

Food

ARTISANAL CHOCOLATES (Bon-Bons or Truffles)

Artisanal chocolates are miniature pieces of artwork crafted from exquisite chocolate—some filled, some solid. They are made to look as exquisite as they taste. Each piece should be appreciated and enjoyed as a delicacy. Frame these miniature pieces of artwork by displaying on a mirror or large frame in a grid-like fashion so guests can admire their beauty before they indulge. *Partybluprints Pick: Truffles— CocoLuxe Fine Pastries, Peapack, N.J. (pictured), or Bon-Bons (50 piece box)—Jacques Torres Chocolate Haven, N.Y., N.Y.*

Materials
50 pieces artisanal chocolates

Structural Notes
❖ On a large mirror, frame, or mirrored tray, arrange chocolates in a series of columns and rows. Display on Dessert Buffet Table.
❖ Purchase an interesting variety, and your guests will delight in "oo-ing and aah-ing" over the selection, as they debate which one to choose.

CHOCOLATE ALMOND BARK

A perfect complement to chocolate is something salty. Dark Chocolate Almond Bark strikes just the right balance. Again, your local bakery or sweet shoppe/candy store may be an excellent resource. *Partybluprints Pick: CocoLuxe Fine Pastries, Peapack, N.J., and Jacques Torres Chocolate Haven, N.Y., N.Y.*

Materials
1 lb. dark chocolate almond bark

Structural Notes
❖ Purchase enough bark to display a few large pieces (a chunk of chocolate laced with nuts is mouthwatering), break the remaining bark into individual serving sizes.
❖ Serve in an attractive pedestal plate or bowl.
❖ Display on Dessert Buffet Table.

Food

INTERMEZZO BERRIES

Rich, luscious berries are a refreshing way to cleanse the palate in between chocolate courses. Offer a mini toppings bar comprised of fresh whipped cream, chocolate fudge, and pastry shells or chocolate bowls.

Materials

3 (6 oz.) containers of blackberries
3 (6 oz.) containers of raspberries
3 (16 oz.) containers of strawberries
3 (6 oz.) containers of blueberries

1 jar chocolate fudge sauce
45 mini pastry shells or 20 regular
   sized (optional: 20 chocolate bowls)

Structural Notes

❖ Wash and dry berries. Gently mix together and refrigerate until ready to serve.
❖ Serve in a footed glass/crystal bowl with the following sides:
   • fresh whipped cream served in a footed glass/crystal bowl or a glass/crystal bowl,
   • chocolate fudge sauce served in a small glass/crystal bowl, and
   • pastry shells or chocolate bowls—use in lieu of bowls.
❖ Create an Intermezzo Berry Station or serve on your buffet table if you have room.

FRESH WHIPPED CREAM

Nothing looks or tastes as dreamy as fresh whipped cream. This "light" heavenly topping provides perfect contrast to the "darkness" of the evening.

Materials

1 quart heavy cream
½ cup confectioners' sugar
2 teaspoons vanilla

Structural Notes

❖ Chill a stainless steel mixing bowl and beaters in the freezer for thirty minutes.
❖ Add one quart heavy cream, whip on high speed until stiff peaks begin to form (about four to five minutes), then gradually add ½ cup confectioners' sugar (add more for desired sweetness) and two teaspoons of vanilla.
❖ Refrigerate until ready to serve.

Food

CHOCOLATE TASTING BAR

For many, dark chocolate holds the same promise as a new wine.
A Chocolate Tasting is an easy way to get guests to mingle and converse.
Partybluprints Picks: Here are our best of the best chocolate recommendations in differing price ranges:
> *Jacques Torres Chocolate Haven Bar Single Origin Peru 64% Cocoa, Jacques Torres Chocolate Haven, N.Y., N.Y.,*
> *Perugina Bittersweet Signature Dark Chocolate 60% Cocoa—check local stores,*
> *Vosges, Haute Chocolat, Red Fire Bar, 55% Cacao, Exotic Candy Bar, Vosges Haute Chocolate, N.Y., N.Y., and*
> *Hershey's Cacao Reserve Extra Dark Chocolate 65% Cacao—check local stores.*

Materials
8 dark chocolate bars (select 4 different varieties and purchase 2 of each)

Structural Notes
❖ The Chocolate Tasting Bar should be displayed in its own special place.
❖ Make copies of the included "Chocolate Tasting Rating Sheet" for each guest, instructions are included.
❖ Choose type of tasting:
  a. Blind Tasting: The "identity" is concealed. This prevents any bias/preconceptions from "weighing in" on the tasting experience. When guests have tasted, rated, and compared notes, reveal the "identities" of your chocolate selections.
  b. Open Tasting: Simply label each chocolate, conduct tasting, rate, and compare notes.
❖ Break chocolate bars into bite-sized squares—perfect for tasting. Group them by variety on a mirror/tray or display in a segmented serving dish. Label each group with a place tile or marker—check local craft stores. If you are doing a blind taste testing, label chocolate with a number instead of a name (remember to make a note to yourself matching the number to the name of the chocolate).
❖ Familiarize yourself with the chocolate tasting instructions by taking a test run.
❖ Although a Chocolate Tasting is a great tool to create interaction among your guests, you also have the option to forego a formal tasting and allow guests to taste at their leisure.

BUILDER'S NOTE: *Arrange an area next to the Tasting Bar containing the Chocolate Tasting Sheets and pens.*

Food

LIQUID CHOCOLATE SHOTS

As your guests sip liquid chocolate, they might just have
an out of body experience. Easily whip up this liquid chocolate
and put the food of the gods on your guests' lips.
*Partybluprints Pick: Jacques Torres Wicked Hot Chocolate mix,
Jacques Torres Chocolate Haven, N.Y., N.Y.*

Materials
1 (18 oz.) container Jacques Torres Wicked Hot Chocolate
  (if you substitute a different brand, make a comparable
  substitution with comparable ingredients)
5 cups 2% milk

Structural Notes
❖ Prepare Wicked Hot Chocolate according to directions on the tin.
  Serve immediately in demitasse cups. If using another type of serving container
  (glass, cup, mug), make sure it can handle the heat of the liquid chocolate.
❖ Beware: A little goes a long way. A serving is only a few sips—it really is liquid
  chocolate, not typical hot chocolate.
❖ Use your best serving tray to pass around this decadent specialty, the food
  of the gods.

COFFEE (OPTIONAL STATION)

Cap off the evening with a cup of coffee. The darkness of the coffee
is a testament to the richness of the evening.

Materials
1 lb. coffee
Cream
Sugar

Structural Notes
❖ Set up coffee maker before party begins.
❖ Brew when preparing Liquid Chocolate Shots.

Special Touches

Music

Music is a must at any party. It is an essential element in creating the vibe—its absence is always noticed. Prepare a music mix ahead of time (playlist on iPod, mix on CD, etc.) to coordinate with the mood of the party. This party calls for a sensual, sultry, and soulful mix of artists coming together to bring you to a place you will not soon forget. Feature Corrine Bailey Rae, KT Tunstall, Joss Stone, Macy Gray, Joe Cocker, Ray Charles, and Gnarls Barkley as your headliners. Your music mix should add to the vibe, while making you feel oh so good.

Partybluprints Pick:
Partybluprints iTunes iMix, visit
www.partybluprintsblog.com and click
on "Book Links" category at the top of
the homepage for details. Reminder:
you can also find all the links for the
Partybluprints Picks here.

Structural Notes
❖ Create a music mix specifically designed to coordinate with the vibe for this party.
❖ Set up sound system ahead of time and make sure it is fully functional.
❖ Make sure music is playing when guests arrive.
❖ Dial into a good balance—not too loud, not too soft. Music should enhance and not detract from, other elements.
❖ Whether you saved your music to a playlist or CD, continue to enjoy it. Every time you play it, you will rekindle the spirit of the evening.

Special Activities

The Chocolate Tasting Bar is your activity. See pg. 201 for all the information you need to conduct your own chocolate tasting.

Favors

End your evening on a personal note and send your guests home with a keepsake from the evening. Wrap one or two pieces of candy (bon-bons/truffles and/or dark chocolate almond bark) in a clear cellophane bag or white candy box tied with a ribbon. Trust us—your guests will privately relive the magic of the evening through this special treat.

Structural Notes
❖ Use excess "candy" from display to fill bags/boxes.
❖ At a minimum, you should have as many favors as you had RSVPs (one favor/couple, one favor/single guest). If you opt to give every guest a favor, plan accordingly when purchasing candy and favor containers.
❖ Do not forget to say goodnight to guests with a warm smile, favor in hand.

Footprint

Layout & Detailed Specs

DESIGN BOARD:
RED CARNATIONS EN MASSE, MULTITUDE OF CANDLES,
DECADENT DISPLAY OF DARK CHOCOLATE,
BLACK VELVET, AND ROSE PETALS

THE FOLLOWING ELEMENTS were hand-selected to build the vibe (sensual, self-indulgent, and sophisticated):

> **Red carnations** arranged en masse in glass containers, interspersed throughout the tablescape, provide intense bursts of color. Amidst the candlelight, their plush, velvety appearance takes on an exotic quality in contrast to the dark elements of the table.

> **Candlelight** adds to the sensual qualities inherent in the red flowers and dark chocolate. Bonus: everyone looks radiant in candlelight, and it is an instant mood enhancer.

> **Mouthwatering display of dark chocolate** represents "taking a walk on the dark side," letting go of your troubles, and indulging in dark chocolate of all varieties.

> **Black velvet**, the basic foundation, exudes luxury and elegance.

> **Red rose petals**' rich texture and color add an element of sophistication.

Flow

CREATE AN INTRIGUING FLOW for your Chocolate Soiree by centrally locating your main Dessert Buffet Table and creating more discreet areas where guests may retreat to indulge privately (e.g., The Chocolate Tasting Bar, The Water and Wine Bars, and the Intermezzo Berries Station). This will keep your guests wondering what is around every corner.

Structural Notes

> Walk around your home to determine the flow of your party. Scout out the sites of your various stations.

> The location of your stations will determine the flow of your party. The goal is to provide areas where people can congregate and mingle. Guests should be able to flow effortlessly from one station to another and help themselves at the various stations:

    1. Welcome
    2. Water/Non-Alcoholic Beverage Bar
    3. Wine Bar
    4. Dessert Buffet
    5. Chocolate Tasting Bar
    6. Intermezzo Berry Bar (optional, may include on Dessert Buffet)

> If your guests always seem to congregate in the kitchen, set up all your stations outside the kitchen. Determine if you need to rearrange any furniture or bring in additional seating/tables.

> The goal is to provide areas where people can congregate and mingle. Guests should be able to flow effortlessly from one station to another and help themselves at the various stations.

> It's always considerate to provide several small seating areas for your guests to relax and truly enjoy the vibe of the party. Create "vignettes" by grouping pillows, benches, stools, and small chairs around existing seating areas/cocktail table(s). Make sure your vignettes can seat at least three or four people.

Tablescape

THE DESSERT BUFFET featuring Chocolate Cake, Pots de la Crème, Artisanal Chocolates (Bon-Bons or Truffles), and Chocolate Almond Bark is your wow factor—it should look absolutely mouthwatering. Inspired by the vibe, build a tablescape that enhances your opulent array of dark chocolate and the overall mood. Your sumptuous chocolate feast table will be eyed throughout the night, causing quite a stir.

SCALE 1½" = 1 FT.
DRAWN BY:-
TRACED BY:-
CHECKED BY:-
SKETCH SHEET.
DATE

PARTYBLUPRINTS

HOW TO BUILD A TABLESCAPE

1. Inventory Materials

2. Build Foundation

3. Add Structural Elements

4. Decorate

Tablescape Materials List

INCLUDED IN COMPREHENSIVE MATERIALS LIST

USE THESE MATERIALS TO CREATE YOUR TABLESCAPE:

> Black velvet 18" wide x 54" long
(long enough to drape over width of table)
> Variety of glass/crystal candlesticks/candelabras/votives
> Tapers, votives, pillar candles
(you can go all white or incorporate red and gold)
> Low glass rectangular vase
or 2 6x6x6 glass cube vases
> Glass cube vases 4x4x4 (6–8)
> Red carnations
> Cake pedestal
> Mirror/mirrored tray for artisanal chocolate
and chocolate tasting (2)
> Crystal bowl/footed bowl (2)
> Interesting serving pieces
> Rose petals

Structural Notes

1. INVENTORY YOUR MATERIALS

Take your Materials List (included at end of plan), and go on a scavenger hunt in your home. Stick with a clear (glass/crystal), white, black, gold/brass palette, and do not forget your vintage stuff. Select a "staging" area near your table. Deposit all items you have collected there. Then, "play" with the items and arrange them until you have built your tablescape. Store unused items.

2. BUILD FOUNDATION

Drape a narrow black velvet tablecloth/fabric over the center of the table (horizontally). This anchors the centerpiece and gives off a luxurious feel in contrast to the natural beauty of a wood table. This also works with a glass table. If you have a table that needs to be completely covered, use a black tablecloth. Lit by candlelight, black velvet creates a very adult and elegant foundation for the tablescape.

3. ADD STRUCTURAL ELEMENTS

Candlesticks | Candelabras and single candlesticks set in groups make a beautiful presentation. Make sure they are of varying heights to accentuate the mood. Avoid displaying them in a symmetrical fashion, as varying heights and groupings always create more visual interest in a tablescape.

Votives | This key element is only effective with a multitude of candles positioned throughout the tablescape (and party areas). Weave votives throughout table in a continuous "s" shape. This creates a visually striking effect. Elsewhere, cluster votive candles in groups of three. You will need a lot of candles to create this look and provide the necessary light. Buy in bulk, 4 to 6 dozen, at your local craft store or online, making sure to get both the glass votive candleholders and votive candles. *Safety Tip: Don't place candles near edge of table or in direct path of guests' reach.*

Flowers | Work centerpiece vase into central location and satellite square cube vases throughout. To build your floral centerpiece and satellite arrangements:
> **Centerpiece:** cut stems of 18 to

24 carnations to height of container—heads of flowers should sit just above edge of container. Line inside of vase with green leaf cut to fit height of vase. Fill container ½ full with water. Tightly gather carnations and place in low rectangular glass vase (you can also use two 6x6x6 glass cube vases and place them side-by-side so they appear as one). Arrangement should be tightly packed with flowers, with no space existing between flowers. They should appear as one.

For the smaller satellite arrangements: follow same procedure using a fraction of flowers to create the same effect in 4x4x4 glass cubes vases.

Serving pieces | Do not add food at this stage. Simply position the following serving pieces:

> **Cake pedestal**—anchor one end of your table with display for your cake.

> **Large mirror**—to be used as a display tray to showcase artisanal chocolates. Arrange chocolates in grid-like pattern, just as they are arranged in a gift box.
> **Extra crystal candlesticks**—instead of inserting taper, top with an artisanal chocolate for added visual interest.
> **Footed glass/crystal bowls**—to serve almond bark, berries, whipped cream and chocolate fudge.
> **Appetizer/dessert dishes**—place at one end of the table along with the flatware and cocktail napkins.
> **Interesting serving pieces**—use pieces that create different levels for displaying desserts. Don't forget utensils, including serving utensils.

4. DECORATE
Add food, floral arrangements, rose petals, and candlelight to Dessert Buffet Table, all other stations, and throughout party area.

LIGHTS OUT IS A MUST!
After you have lit all the candles, dim the lights or turn them off altogether. Everything and everyone should be illuminated by candlelight. Make sure you have your backup supply of votive candles handy in case you need to replace any as the night goes on.

BUILDER'S NOTE: Instructions for setting up your other stations (Welcome, Wine Bar, Water/Non-Alcoholic Bar, Chocolate Tasting Bar, and Intermezzo Berry Bar) are in the Structural Notes sections of Cocktails and Food.

PARTYBLUPRINTS RULE OF GOOD MEASURE

"Always inventory materials before purchasing."

1. Search your home, including storage, for materials.

2. Use your imagination—repurpose items.

3. Borrow.

Architect's Notes

INSIDER'S TIPS

1 **Purchase a gas lighter** with an extender handle. Using matches or a cigarette lighter is cumbersome and time consuming when trying to light a large amount of candles.

2 **Candlelight is essential.** Do not skimp and buy inexpensive tea lights that will not last through the night. Make sure to purchase votive candles instead.

3 **Lighting all the candles** will take longer than you think, so start more than five minutes before guests arrive.

4 **Set out the necessary tools** and premeasured ingredients for the Liquid Chocolate Shots. A host fumbling for pots and recipes during the party can interfere with the mood.

5 **This soiree requires many glasses;** make sure you have enough on hand. Note: If you opt to rent glasses, find a rental company that delivers and will pick up dirty glasses. It's a big time and effort saver.

6 **Buy your bouquet** of roses a few days before the party and enjoy the arrangement before removing petals.

7 **Remember the "U" in Partybluprints** and add your special touches. Bring your "builder's inspiration" to your party by sharing your favorite form of dark chocolate, offering your favorite Cabernet Sauvignon wine that pairs perfectly with dark chocolate, adding some of your favorite songs that fit the vibe into the music mix, or personalizing a favor for your guests with a "goodnight note."

8 **The preparation for this party** is as pleasing as the star of the evening. Everything, with the exception of the liquid chocolate (which takes five minutes to prepare), can be made or purchased prior to the party and can be displayed in advance of your first guest arriving. This leaves you with plenty of time to luxuriously prepare yourself (mentally and physically) for this very special evening.

Materials List

USE THE INCLUDED MATERIALS LIST as your inventory and shopping list all in one. Simply make a copy and check off items you have before doing any shopping. Then, as you shop, continue to inventory items until all materials are "in-house."

Be efficient and keep an updated copy of your list with you whenever you go shopping and update it in real time. This avoids over purchasing and last minute impulse shopping (we like to call it "panic purchasing"), resulting in unnecessary stress and expenditures.

Critical Path

FOLLOW THE INCLUDED CRITICAL PATH to manage your time and tasks so you are not overwhelmed or unprepared for your guests. This guide combines your to-do list and timeline for efficient and effective preparation and execution. We've removed the guesswork and streamlined the process. If you stick to the Party Plan, you can prepare everything ahead of time and be a guest at your own party. What a sweet reward for a job well done!

CHOCOLATE TASTING RATING SHEET

INSTRUCTIONS:

1. Taste lightest to darkest chocolate (just like wine).
2. Press piece of chocolate to the roof of your mouth and hold it there with your tongue. Resist the urge to bite the chocolate. Allow it to relinquish itself.
3. Close your eyes and visualize the chocolate surrounded by the heat of your mouth.
4. Allow the melted chocolate to flow over the sides of your tongue and down your throat.
5. Based on a 1–5 scale (1 highest, 5 lowest), record the results of your sensory experience.
6. Cleanse palate with water in between samples.

CHOCOLATE TASTING RATING					
SAMPLE #/NAME	Aroma	Texture	Flavor	Aftertaste	Overall Experience

BUILDER'S NOTE: You can leave these tasting sheets as is or embellish them to your liking. You may choose to mount on cardstock on a single page or in the middle of a fold-over note card.

PARTYBLUPRINTS CHOCOLATE SOIREE
MATERIALS LIST
SHOPPING LIST FOR 20

- [ ] 4 (750ml) bottles Prosecco
- [ ] 15 (750ml) bottles Cabernet Sauvignon
- [ ] 3 (1 liter) bottles sparkling water
- [ ] 3 (2 liter) bottles soda
- [ ] 1 lb. coffee
- [ ] cream
- [ ] sugar
- [ ] 50 pieces artisanal chocolate (bon-bons or truffles or a combination of the two)
- [ ] 1 container Jacques Torres Wicked Hot Chocolate
- [ ] 1 container Jacques Torres Classic Hot Chocolate
- [ ] 7½ cups 2% milk
- [ ] 1 lb. dark chocolate almond bark
- [ ] 1 jar chocolate fudge sauce
- [ ] 1 dark chocolate bar
- [ ] 8 dark chocolate bars (4 different varieties, 2 of each)
- [ ] 1 large chocolate cake
- [ ] 2 (10 oz.) containers assorted salted nuts
- [ ] 1 (24 oz.) bag pretzel crisps
- [ ] 3 packages mini pastry shells (15/package) or 20 regular size or 20 chocolate bowls
- [ ] 9 pieces citrus fruit (3 each orange, lemon, and lime)
- [ ] 3 (6 oz.) containers of raspberries
- [ ] 3 (6 oz.) containers of blackberries
- [ ] 3 (6 oz.) containers of blueberries
- [ ] 3 (16 oz.) containers of strawberries
- [ ] 1 quart heavy cream
- [ ] ½ cup confectioners' sugar
- [ ] 2 tsp. vanilla
- [ ] votive candles (bulk/4–6 dozen)
- [ ] 6 tapers (or as needed)
- [ ] 4–6 pillar candles
- [ ] 4–6 dozen red carnations
- [ ] 1 dozen large green leaves
- [ ] 1 dozen red roses
- [ ] 1 18"(w) x 54"(l) black velvet fabric/black tablecloth
- [ ] variety of glass/crystal candlesticks/candelabras/votives
- [ ] 1 low glass rectangular vase or 2 6x6x6 glass cube cases
- [ ] 6–8 glass cube vases 4x4x4
- [ ] cake pedestal
- [ ] 2 mirrors/mirrored trays for artisanal chocolate and chocolate tasting
- [ ] 2 crystal bowls/footed bowls
- [ ] interesting serving pieces
- [ ] favor boxes/bags
- [ ] stemware (flutes, wine and water glasses) and coffee cups
- [ ] flatware and dessert plates
- [ ] napkins
- [ ] ice and ice bucket

NOTES

PARTYBLUPRINTS CHOCOLATE SOIREE
CRITICAL PATH
TIMELINE/TO-DO LIST

Requires Immediate Attention

- [ ] Choose the date for your Chocolate Soiree.
- [ ] Create a guest list.
- [ ] Send out invitations.
- [ ] Determine what items you have in stock (accessories, tableware, serving pieces).
- [ ] Order items you need well in advance of your party.

The Week before the Party

- [ ] Walk around your home to determine the flow of your party. Scout the site of your various stations.
- [ ] Test your sound system and create your music mix/burn CD.
- [ ] Inventory items for the party and purchase any products still needed.

One to Two Days before the Party

- [ ] Shop for any last minute items (e.g., berries, flowers).
- [ ] Prepare Pots de la Crème and refrigerate.
- [ ] Print out the Menu included in this Partybluprints Party Plan, frame it and display it.

One Day before the Party

- [ ] Create floral centerpiece and several satellite arrangements.
- [ ] Layout tablescape by setting out flowers, serving dishes, votives, candlesticks, candelabras, flatware, dishes, and napkins.
- [ ] Set up your "Welcome to the Evening Station" minus the Prosecco and sparkling water, which should be chilling.
- [ ] Set up the Wine Bar. Be mindful of the location; your guests will congregate at this location upon arriving.
- [ ] Display favors somewhere by the front door so you won't forget to give them to your guests as they leave.
- [ ] If it's coat weather, clear a space in your hall closet or other designated location for your guests' coats.
- [ ] Take some time in your closet to choose an outfit in which you look and feel fantastic!

Day of the Party

- [ ] Start the day off on a good note; it's the day of your party!
- [ ] Designate a time to get yourself ready and stick to it.
- [ ] Have a cup of coffee or whatever gets you going and start the final preparations for your party!

Four Hours before the Party

- [ ] Prepare fresh whipped cream and refrigerate.

- [ ] Rinse berries, let them drip dry in colander, refrigerate.
- [ ] Measure out Liquid Chocolate Shots ingredients and organize tools.
- [ ] Arrange Artisanal Chocolates (Bon-Bons/Truffles).
- [ ] Display Chocolate Almond Bark.
- [ ] Set up Intermezzo Berries Station minus the berries and whipped cream.
- [ ] Set up Chocolate Tasting Bar.
- [ ] Set up coffee station. Get coffee maker all ready so all you have to do later is push the start button.

Two Hours before the Party

- [ ] Remember the "U" in Partybluprints and add your special touches, if you haven't already.
- [ ] You followed the Partybluprints Party Plan and physically prepared the party, now it's time to prepare you. Shower and dress in something that makes you feel great. Let the excitement of your party envelop you.

One Hour before the Party

- [ ] Remove refrigerated items and place at appropriate stations/tablescape (Chocolate Cake, Pots de la Crème, berries, whipped cream).
- [ ] Set up Water Bar.
- [ ] Sprinkle rose petals everywhere you want your guests to roam.
- [ ] Open a few bottles of Cabernet and let them breathe.

Thirty Minutes before the Party

- [ ] Start lighting all the votives and candles (it may take you a little longer than you think).

Fifteen Minutes before the Party

- [ ] Start the music.
- [ ] Dim the lights.
- [ ] Take a walk around, admire your work, and feel the vibe.
- [ ] Pop the Prosecco, pour yourself a glass, and toast yourself for a job well done!
- [ ] Pour Prosecco and sparkling water into flutes at Welcome Station.

One and a Half Hours into the Party

- [ ] Make the Liquid Chocolate Shots. Remember, this is the food of the gods, so use your best serving tray to pass this decadent specialty. This is the perfect opportunity to personally check in with your guests.
- [ ] Brew coffee.
- [ ] Now stop and take in the moment you have created and gifted to your guests and yourself.

BEHIND THE BLUPRINT —OUR PARTY NOTES

WE WERE INSPIRED TO CREATE THE WHAT A GIRL WANTS PARTY PLAN BECAUSE, after attending countless "in home" shopping parties, we knew that there had to be a better way to host one. Many times, we felt flat after leaving a shopping party because it was all shopping and no party. After we had purchased our products, we felt it was time to go. With all the effort that goes into planning a shopping party on the part of the host and the salesperson, it only makes sense to make the most of it. With a bit more planning, you get both a shopping party and a party.

Oh boy (girl), did we have a blast at our What a Girl Wants party! Our charity of choice for the night was Susan G. Komen for the Cure. Since the party was for women and the cause to eradicate breast cancer is dear to our hearts, we wanted to give this party a purpose, and we love the idea of giving a portion of the proceeds to a charity. To make the night special, we turned Dawn's home into a unique boutique for the night, treating our gal pals to cocktails, fancy nibbles, and shopping in a "Girls' World" we created just for them. With all these wonderful women attending, we wanted to give them a reason to stay and play! The addition of music, a cocktail, and some bite-size treats turned shopping into a party! Since there were so many women at the party, we decided to splurge and hire a bartender for the night. It was great having a handsome man serving the ladies all night!

The vibe of this party owes a lot to the music. It really gets everyone in the mood. Our spin on shopping was made special by 1154 LILL Studio. Our gal pals were able to design their own handbags that night, and those who didn't wish to do so had fun helping others pick out fabric and designs. Everyone had a blast mingling and noshing on treats. As our final nod to breast cancer awareness, we sent each of our friends home with Cookies for a Cure from Cheryl&Co.® as a favor and a reminder to schedule checkups.

Celebrate
Your "Inner" Girl

WHAT A GIRL WANTS

SCINTILLATE THE SENSES by hosting a luxurious party full of heavenly scents, calming pink nuances, and "feel good" music mixed with shopping! This sophisticated party allows women to shop 'til they drop while sipping chic champagne, nibbling on dainty delights, delving into decadent desserts, and lounging in the lap of luxury with friends. What more could a girl want?

Is your "inner girl" repressed, forgotten, or just yearning to bask in her own brilliant light? Let her loose and celebrate her spirit. Gather your "girlfriends" and treat them to a fabulous evening out in a "girls' world" you've created just for them.

VIBE
√ Feminine
√ Fancy
√ Fabulous

Review Party Plan

YOUR SET OF BLUPRINTS

THE PARTYBLUPRINTS WHAT A GIRL WANTS PARTY PLAN is an evening party that is sure to delight your girlfriends. This plan gives girlfriends the time and space to connect, have fun, and enjoy their favorite things—together. Your Party Plan, a thoroughly coordinated "bluprint," details the concept, design, materials, and methods. We've put all the essential information and helpful tools at your fingertips. Simply follow your set of bluprints (Party Plan) and start building your party now.

SCALE 1½" = 1 Ft.
DRAWN By:-
TRACED By:-
CHECKED BY:-

SKETCH SHEET.

DATE

PARTYBLUPRINTS = ARCHITECT
YOU = BUILDER

This Party Plan is your set of "bluprints"
for building your party.
You are the "U" in Partybluprints.

Your set of bluprints contains the following:

SCOPE & CORE ELEMENTS (Concept & Foundation)

SPECS (Party Components)

FOOTPRINT (Layout, Detailed Specs, Flow & Tablescape)

ARCHITECT'S NOTES (Insider's Tips)

MATERIALS LIST (Shopping List)

CRITICAL PATH (Timeline/To-Do List)

Scope & Core Elements
CONCEPT & FOUNDATION

Cocktails, Fancy Nibbles, and Shopping
+ Feminine, Fancy, and Fabulous
= What a Girl Wants

THIS EVENING IS ALL ABOUT TAKING THE TIME TO INDULGE in all things feminine, fancy, and fabulous. What could be better than sipping an inviting cocktail, trying some new culinary delights, and going shopping at an intimate boutique—all with your closest girlfriends in tow? With shopping as your activity, transform your home into a unique boutique that appeals to any guest and sets a chic vibe. Tell your guests to put on their rose-colored glasses and reconnect with their inner girl. After you create this magic, you and your girlfriends will remember just how good it is to be a girl.

Create a "Girls' World"

WHO	Women Only
WHAT	Cocktail Party
WHERE	Your Home
WHEN	Late Afternoon or Evening
WHY	To Spend Time with the Girls
HOW	Follow Bluprint

Specs

PARTY COMPONENTS

WE BELIEVE the most effective and enjoyable approach to entertaining is to start with a plan that stimulates all five senses. There are six key party components in every PARTYBLUPRINTS PARTY PLAN:

Invitations   Cocktails   Food

Music   Special Activities   Favors

Pay attention to all the components of your party and make sure they enhance, and do not detract, from one another. Consider this party a symphony for the senses: vision, palate, aroma, acoustics, and feeling. If you achieve the right balance, your guests' senses will be satisfied, resulting in relaxed, happy guests and the perfect party environment!

Invitations

Whether you send handwritten, printed or electronic invitations, make sure they are pretty in PINK. If you are featuring a vendor who's donating a percentage of sales to a designated charity, let your guests know in the invitation. It will add to the spirit of the party. Also, include a fun note like, "Wear Your Favorite Shoes" or "Bring on the Bling."

Please join us for a

What a Girl Wants

Cocktails, Fancy Nibbles & Shopping Party

On
May 22, 2010 / 8pm
At the home of
Ann Lorelli / 1532 Meade Ave.
RSVP to
Ann Lorelli
305 555 3544 / ann @ lorelli.com
By
May 18, 2010

Now that you've invited your guests, it's time to plan your menu. Here are our Partybluprints Picks:

What a Girl Wants

Menu

Cocktails

Rose Royale
French Beaujolais Wine

Fancy Nibbles

Apple and Brie Crostini
Potato Nests with Sour Cream and Toppings
Belgian Endive BLT
Tarlettes with Roasted Red Pepper and Goat Cheese
Roast Beef Croustades with Horseradish

Desserts

Strawberry and Chocolate Spoonfuls
Double Chocolate Brownie Bites

Cocktails

ROSE ROYALE—SIGNATURE COCKTAIL

Tonight's cocktail will show your guests how fabulous the world looks through rose-colored glasses, namely their cocktail glass!

Brut Rosé Sparkling Wine is our "it" bubbly of the evening. "Accessorize" your signature cocktail with an exquisite edible crystallized sweetheart rose and send the message to the ladies that they are "it." Since this cocktail is absolutely a royal treat, it should be given a place of honor as the welcoming cocktail. What woman is not instantly overcome by a festive mood when given some pink bubbly? This is the ultimate drink for making a girl feel special, just like she wants.

Partybluprints Picks: French Brut Rosé Sparkling Wines: Lucien Albrecht Cremant d'Alsace Brut Rosé or Charles de Fére Brut Rosé. Both are excellent choices and values for a perfect glass of dry pink bubbly!
If this wine is not available locally, try online resources.
Edible crystallized flowers: Sweetfields, Jamul, Calif.

Materials
7 bottles French Brut Rosé Sparkling Wine
40 edible crystallized sweetheart roses

Structural Notes
❖ Simply pour a glass of sparkling wine and top with an edible crystallized sweetheart rose, hence Rose Royale.
❖ Rule of thumb: One (750 ml) bottle of sparkling wine serves six. We recommend seven bottles; you will definitely get some women wanting a second glass of pink bubbly!
❖ Have a Rose Royale cocktail ready for each guest as they step through the front door.

Set up a "Rose" Bar/ Welcome Station featuring the Rose Royale—the star of this bar.

> Think about the location of your Rose Bar. It will be a gathering spot as your guests arrive. This station will be active and should be feminine and functional. The Rose Bar will be your guests' first stop where they will discover a few treasures: edible crystallized sweetheart roses, French Brut Rosé Sparkling Wine, and French Beaujolais Wine.

> If you do not have a bar or free counter, a six-foot rectangular table is perfect for the foundation of your Rose Bar. Once you've established your bar, drape it with a white tablecloth.

> Anchor one side of the bar with pretty crystal buckets or other pretty containers filled with sparkling wine on ice. Refrigerate remaining bottles. Fill in this side with champagne flutes. Anchor the other side with your supply of Beaujolais and red wine glasses.

> Place some flowers (you can use one or more rose votives—see pg. 260 for more information) in your party's signature colors on the Rose Bar along with votive candles.

> Sprinkle rose petals around the base of your vase and candles.

> Display exquisite edible crystallized flowers on a fancy tray or in a glass jar so they are one of the first things your guests spy when arriving at the Rose Bar. How luxurious to have such an exquisite "accessory" in a cocktail.

FRENCH BEAUJOLAIS WINE

After your guests have enjoyed a fancy cocktail, treat them to a glass of French Beaujolais Wine. Just saying Beaujolais, "bō-zhō-lā," makes you feel giddy.
Partybluprints Picks: French Beaujolais Wine: Georges DuBoeuf "Domaine Jean Descombes" Morgon or "Domaine des Rosier" Moulin-a-Vent. If this wine is not available locally, try an online resource.

Materials
10 bottles French Beaujolais

Structural Notes
❖ As the women finish their cocktail (some will be done after one glass, others may wish to continue on with a second), trade them their empty glass for a glass of Beaujolais.

❖ Tip from Kirk Sprenger, our Resident Wine Expert: "The unique thing about Beaujolais is that it is the one red wine that can truly be drunk cold. However, I would still serve it at 'cellar temperature,' which is about 55–65 degrees. It does not need much breathing time at all because it has a very light and fruity style that opens up easily."

❖ As previously mentioned, the Beaujolais will be set up at the opposite end of the Rose Bar from the signature cocktail. Set up your glasses here also with a few bottles of Beaujolais on ice and a few open and ready to pour. Remember the suggested temperature is 55–65 degrees, so place them on ice one hour before guests' arrival.

EXPERT COMMENTARY

Kirk Sprenger, Wine Expert and Proprietor of The Chappaqua Wine & Spirit Company, Chappaqua, N.Y.

FRENCH BRUT ROSÉ SPARKLING WINE

When asked why I prefer a Rosé over a regular Brut, my answer quite simply is that a Rosé has a bit more elegance, a bit more flavor, and overall a better feel in the mouth. They most frequently are produced from Pinot Noir grapes, one of my personal favorites.

FRENCH BEAUJOLAIS

When the girls get together and are in that "zone of their own," the atmosphere is always the same—fun. Whether it's a ladies' luncheon, girls' night out, or a shopping party, the one thing to remember is to keep it light; that includes the food and the wine. What better way to keep it light and fun than to serve up Beaujolais from France? Everyone knows the Beaujolais Nouveau that arrives the third Thursday of November every year, but, truth be told, the Beaujolais that are with us throughout the rest of the year are delicious values. They are comprised of Gamay grapes: bright purple in

color, fruitful and low in tannins, the perfect equation for a fun wine. Because of their reputation for being drunk in a casual mode, they are one of the few reds that are fashionably acceptable to drink chilled. Beaujolais Villages and the ten premium towns, known as Cru's, are full of life and refreshing. These ten towns are given the privilege of carrying their name on the label and can be identified as: Brouilly, Cote de Brouilly, Saint Amour, Chenas, Chiroubles, Fleurie, Julienas, Morgon, Moulin-a-Vent, and Regnie, the newest to enter the fold in 1988. Each of these exhibits their own unique characteristics, from the most delicate Chiroubles to the weightiest style of Moulin-a-Vent, from the violet and floral scents of Saint Amour to the more mineral and spice edges of Morgon.

Perhaps one of the finest examples of pure Beaujolais is George Duboeuf's "Domaine Jean Descombes" Morgon. It is a very exuberant glass of Gamay with an abundance of cherry-rich fruit and a velvety texture. One can see the elegance of this wine through its bright purple hue. If this is unavailable, as it is from time to time, try seeking out Georges Duboeuf's "Domaine des Rosier" Moulin-a-Vent. This is a very close equivalent that shows an abundance of fresh, ripe berry fruit with a good backbone.

BUILDER'S NOTE: If you have not established a relationship with a local wine proprietor, seek out some experts by visiting wine shops in your area. Wine experts can be an excellent resource and help you to explore your preferences.

Cocktails

Water/Non-Alcoholic Beverages

Always offer water and some non-alcoholic options at your bar.

Rose Royale Mocktail

For those ladies seeking a non-alcoholic alternative, offer a bubbly Rose Royale Mocktail at your Rose Bar.

Materials
3 six packs club soda or seltzer
1 (32 oz.) container pomegranate juice
3 limes
Edible sweetheart roses

Structural Notes
❖ Before the party, slice fresh limes, refrigerate until ready to use, then display in a pretty crystal or glass bowl.
❖ Fill a champagne flute 3/4 of the way with club soda or seltzer, add a dash of pomegranate juice, a squirt of fresh lime, and top it off with an edible sweetheart rose for an elegant non-alcoholic alternative to the signature cocktail. For guests enjoying a refreshing glass of club soda/seltzer, the lime offers a tart splash.

PARTYBLUPRINTS RULE OF GOOD MEASURE

"Always offer non-alcoholic beverages at your bar and table."

1. Be considerate of your guests—don't assume all your guests drink alcohol.

2. Offer a festive non-alcoholic alternative to your signature cocktail.

3. Support responsible drinking.

INFUSED WATER

For those looking to quench their thirst, give them a visual and tasty treat—exotic berry water. Your guests will be so intrigued that they'll have to take a taste.

Materials
Water
2 (16 oz.) containers strawberries

Structural Notes
❖ Fill glass pitcher or beverage dispenser with water.
❖ Add rinsed and hulled strawberries and let water sit for twenty-four hours.
❖ Refrigerate.
❖ The strawberries will lose their color to the water, so remove strawberries and replace with fresh ones before serving.
❖ If room permits, display at the Rose Bar; otherwise locate infused water near the Main Dining Table or in a special spot of its own.

BUILDER'S NOTE: Finally, no matter how fancy your party, you know there will be some of your friends fishing around for a cold Diet Coke later, so have some iced. Select the single serving fancy bottles as an upgrade to the usual can they are used to drinking out of—they'll appreciate it. This is one of those things that may simply be, "What a Girl Wants!"

FANCY NIBBLES

(Serves 20)

SINCE THIS PARTY IS ALL ABOUT FEMININE, fancy, and fabulous, these slightly delicate "finger foods" are perfect. Your guests will still be able to work the room(s) while enjoying cocktails, food, and shopping—all while wearing a fabulous pair of shoes!

The added bonus is that these Fancy Nibbles are easy to make, a cinch to prepare ahead of time, and are as delicious as they look. Your friends are guaranteed to be delighted that you whipped up such an assortment of luscious treats that look and taste fabulous! The following recipes yield at least two of each Fancy Nibble per guest, and, with five selections, this will allow everyone to create a satisfying plate.

Food

APPLE AND BRIE CROSTINI (Makes 50)

These toasted treats with tart Granny Smith apple slices
and warm Brie are absolutely scrumptious.

Materials
2 large French baguettes
$^1/_2$ cup olive oil
Kosher salt or coarse sea salt to taste
2 Granny Smith apples
1 cup of lemon juice
2 lb. Brie wheel
11 oz. container walnuts

Structural Notes
❖ Preheat the oven to 400 degrees.
❖ Slice the bread on a slight angle into one-inch thick slices.
❖ Arrange sliced bread flat on baking pans in single layers.
❖ Using a pastry brush, brush the top side of each slice with olive oil and sprinkle
  with the coarse sea salt.
❖ Bake in the oven ten to fifteen minutes, until golden brown and crunchy.
  Keep an eye on them so they do not get too well done.
❖ Let cool completely then store in an airtight container up to four days.
❖ Core apples and cut into very thin slices (twenty-five slices per apple.)
❖ Place slices in bowl and toss with lemon juice, making sure to fully coat apples
  to keep them from turning brown.
❖ Heat the Brie in microwave with rind on it, just until softened, 15–25 seconds.
  When softened, remove rind.
❖ Spread Brie on each crostini and top with a slice of apple.
❖ Just before guests arrive, arrange crostini on a glass/crystal/white serving piece
  and display on Main Dining Buffet.
❖ Optional: Prepare another platter with a small wedge or two of Brie, apple slices
  and walnuts (include a knife to slice the Brie)—this offers the ladies the option
  to prepare it the way they want.

Food

POTATO NESTS WITH SOUR CREAM AND TOPPINGS (Makes 48)

This treat is so elegantly packaged, you would never guess it's comfort food. The potato nests are served with sour cream and a selection of toppings: chives, bacon, and caviar (optional). We're not recommending a nest with the works. These selection of toppings offer two options for your guests: (1) a dressed up baked potato or (2) a sophisticated and fresh way to enjoy caviar.

Materials
2 (30 oz.) bags frozen shredded hash brown potatoes, thawed
1 cup onion, finely diced
6 eggs, beaten
Kosher or sea salt
Fresh cracked pepper
2 cups sour cream
1 cup crispy and crumbled bacon
$^1/^3$ cup fresh sliced chives
Optional: 1 oz. caviar (Keep caviar fresh and tasting its best by keeping it on ice. Do not use a metal spoon or bowl when serving or handling caviar.)

Structural Notes
❖ Preheat oven to 400 degrees.
❖ Generously grease mini-muffin tins and set aside.
❖ Drain thawed potatoes in a colander.
❖ In a large bowl, mix together thawed potatoes, onion, and eggs, add salt and pepper to your taste.
❖ For each potato nest, spoon one tablespoon potato mixture into the palm of your hand, form into a ball and squeeze out excess liquid into a separate bowl.
❖ Don't be alarmed by the amount of liquid that is squeezed out. Even though it looks like a lot of egg has been squeezed out, the potato has reserved just enough to bind the nest during baking.
❖ Place ball into a muffin cup and form a cup by pressing your thumb into the middle of the ball, causing the mixture to form the basket.
❖ Repeat steps with the remaining potato mixture.

- ❖ Bake for forty minutes.
- ❖ Remove from oven to cool on a rack. When cooled, cover with foil until ready to fill.
- ❖ Just before guests arrive, arrange nests on glass/crystal/white serving pieces, spoon a dollop of sour cream into each nest and display on Main Dining Table.
- ❖ Serve toppings alongside and allow your guests to personalize their nests with the toppings you have provided.

Food

BELGIAN ENDIVE BLT (Makes 60)

If you can believe it, we have nestled your beloved BLT into an endive spear. It's cute, compact, and easy to enjoy at a cocktail party. Close your eyes when you take a bite and you'll think you are eating a BLT. This is an outrageous, fancy nibble and it will drive your friends crazy—it's so good.

Materials
60 Belgian endive spears
12 plum tomatoes, diced and drained
3 lbs. bacon, cooked and crumbled
3 Tbsp. mayonnaise
1 box garlic croutons, crushed
4 small to medium round red tomatoes

Structural Notes

❖ Separate and wash endive spears. Be sure to completely dry each spear to avoid browning of the edges.
❖ Dice tomatoes and place in strainer to drain excess liquid.
❖ Cook bacon until extra crispy, cool, and crumble.
❖ Place croutons in a sealed plastic bag and crush, not too finely. They should be larger than regular breadcrumbs, about the size of panko breadcrumbs.
❖ Place tomatoes in a bowl and mix in bacon and mayo.
❖ Fill thirty to forty endive spears with one teaspoon bacon and tomato mixture.
❖ Sprinkle with crushed croutons.
❖ Arrange filled endive spears on large round platters (glass, crystal, white) like the petals of a flower. Place one small to medium-sized red tomato in the middle of each platter for the center of the flower. Optional: Place the remaining bacon, tomato and mayo mixture on a different platter with the remaining Belgian endive and croutons—once again, the girls can opt to make it the way they want it.
❖ Display on Main Dining Buffet.

Food

TARTLETTES WITH ROASTED RED PEPPER AND GOAT CHEESE (Makes 60)

These mini fillo (phyllo) shells stuffed with roasted red pepper and topped with goat cheese are the perfect combination of tastes and textures rolled into one.

Materials
3 packages mini fillo shells (15/box)
2 (4 oz.) logs plain goat cheese
1 (12 oz.) container roasted red peppers, rinsed, drained and diced

Structural Notes
❖ If shells are frozen, thaw according to package directions.
❖ Fill halfway with diced roasted red pepper and top with crumbled plain goat cheese.
❖ Just before guests arrive, arrange on glass/crystal/white serving pieces and display on Main Dining Buffet.

Food

ROAST BEEF CROUSTADES WITH HORSERADISH (Makes 48)

Roast beef tucked into a toasted bread cup and topped with fresh horseradish and a fresh bit of parsley is "delicately" satisfying.

Materials
2 loaves sliced white bread
$1/2$ stick of butter
1 lb. very thinly sliced rare deli roast beef
Coarse sea salt
1 cup fresh horseradish
1 bunch fresh Italian parsley

Structural Notes
❖ Preheat oven to 350 degrees.
❖ Lightly grease mini-muffin tins with butter and set aside.
❖ Cut crusts from bread; roll each slice very thin with rolling pin.
❖ Cut each piece of bread into four equal squares.
❖ Lay a square of bread centered over each muffin opening and press neatly and evenly into mini-muffin tins.
❖ Bake for ten minutes or until lightly brown.
❖ Cool completely and store in an airtight container for up to two days.
❖ Fill each croustade with approximately $1/4$ to $1/2$ of a slice of roast beef, sprinkle lightly with sea salt, top with a dollop of fresh horseradish and a leaf of Italian parsley as a garnish.
❖ Arrange croustades on a glass/crystal/white serving piece and display on Main Dining Buffet.

Food

DESSERTS

While it is said that some people are born with a silver spoon in their mouth, we've decided to give all the ladies a privileged feeling tonight. All the desserts are served in Chinese soup spoons. The presentation is fancy and fabulous, and how fun to indulge in a guilty pleasure in one bite. To give the ladies an excuse to indulge in two desserts, we had to add some fruit. Plus, both desserts feature a girl's second best friend—chocolate! Create one of each Chinese soup spoon desserts for each guest.

Partybluprint Pick: Chinese Porcelain Soup Spoons—Amazon.com or try your local kitchen supply store.

STRAWBERRY AND CHOCOLATE SPOONFULS

Who doesn't love chocolate-covered strawberries? We refined this favorite a bit for a more sophisticated presentation. On a bed of chocolate sauce lies a strawberry. Everything is fair game, especially double dipping!

Materials
20 long-stemmed strawberries (wash and thoroughly dry)
1 jar chocolate sauce

Structural Notes
❖ Arrange Chinese soup spoons on a large tray.
❖ Pour chocolate sauce into a spouted measuring cup and fill each soup spoon with just enough sauce to cover the bottom of the spoon. If you pour too much, when you place the strawberry on top, the sauce will overflow.
❖ Place one long-stemmed strawberry in the center of every spoon.
❖ Transport to dessert table and arrange spoons on one end of the dessert table. Whether you choose to display your spoons in an array (columns and rows) or arcs (cascading semi-circles), be consistent and arrange the Brownie Bites (see pg. 260) in the same pattern on the other end of the table. Make sure all handles are facing in the same direction, outward, so guests can easily pick them up.
❖ If long-stemmed strawberries are not available at your local market or supermarket, you may substitute regular strawberries.

Food

DOUBLE CHOCOLATE BROWNIE BITES (*Yields:* 22)

What a girl wants and deserves is a brownie. The best part of a brownie is always the first bite, so let your guests savor this bite-size gooey chocolatey brownie topped with a raspberry. Present the Brownie Bite on a Chinese soup spoon and send the ladies over the moon!

Materials

1 package brownie mix (use double chocolate or chocolate chunk)
$^1/_3$ cup oil*
1 egg*
2 (6 oz.) containers raspberries, washed and dried
20 mint leaves
* *May need to adjust these amounts according to your boxed brownie mix instructions.*

Structural Notes

❖ Purchase double chocolate brownie mix (use a mix with chocolate chunks to make your brownie bites even more delectable), or, if you want, make your own from scratch.
❖ Follow mixing instructions as per the box or recipe.
❖ Instead of cooking brownies in a pan, cook in mini-muffin tins. This will create the perfect bite-size brownie!
❖ Generously grease tins and fill each well almost to the top.
❖ Cook for fifteen minutes at 325 degrees.
❖ Let the brownies cool. If not serving immediately, store in airtight container.
❖ Arrange Chinese soup spoons on a large tray.
❖ Place each brownie bite on a Chinese soup spoon and top with a fresh raspberry and a mint leaf.
❖ Transport to dessert table and arrange spoons in array form (rows and columns) or arcs (see pg. 260 for details). Make sure all handles are facing in the same direction, outward, so guests can easily pick them up.

COFFEE

In a separate area, such as a kitchen counter, set up coffee service. This is a great spot to offer guests their favors in a basket alongside the coffee.

Materials
1 lb. coffee
Sugar
Cream

Structural Notes
❖ Set up coffee maker before party begins and brew.
❖ Brew coffee one hour into party.

Special Touches

Music

A soulful, spiritual, and sensational mix of artists is what a girl wants, really! Create a music mix that is the perfect enhancement for your party. Feature a combination of India.Arie, Colbie Caillat, Christina Aguilera, and Sara Bareilles to celebrate the spirit of this party.

Partybluprints Pick:
Partybluprints iTunes iMix, visit www.partybluprintsblog.com and click on "Book Links" category at the top of the home page for details. Reminder: you can also find all the links for the Partybluprints Picks here.

Special Activities

Invite your guests to indulge in a favorite activity, shopping. Transform your home into a unique boutique that appeals to any guest. They will feel special, sophisticated, and pampered. There are so many "in-home" shopping options: clothing, jewelry, home accessories, skin-care products, etc.

BUILDER'S NOTE: You may substitute any function for shopping. This party is perfect for a Girls' Night that features fundraisers, lecture/guest speaker, club meetings, or simply socializing!

Favors

Send your guests home with a favor that pays tribute to your designated charity. In support of breast cancer awareness, we treated our guests to pink-frosted heart cookies. Bake cut-out sugar cookies in the shape of a heart or an awareness ribbon (cookie cutters are widely available online or try your local kitchen supply store) and then frost them in your chosen charity's color. Wrap each cookie in a cellophane bag and tie with a ribbon in the same color as the frosting. This is a great way to send guests home with a homemade treat and a message.

Footprint

Layout & Detailed Specs

THIS EVENING IS ALL ABOUT RECONNECTING with how good it feels to be a girl and indulging in being feminine, fancy, and fabulous!

These basic elements combine to create a vibe that is perfect for socializing with the girls while doing some shopping.

> **Flowers |** Bright pink roses and Granny Smith Apple green flowers—this dynamic color combination is the perfect balance of sophisticated elegance and sheer fun. When you look at these colors, you cannot help but feel lively and happy.

> **Candles |** Everything (and everyone) looks better in candlelight; naturally candles are a must.

> **Touches of Gold |** Display candles on gold (brass) dishes for a dash of sparkle—girls love sparkle.

> **Fancy Nibbles |** The focus of this tablescape is the finger food. Display an array of specialties for big impact—you'll have a professional-looking presentation that you created yourself! Won't the girls be proud.

Flow

FOR THIS PARTY, recreate the exciting shopping experience of discovering new departments and displays within a store or boutique by creating four distinct "departments" for your boutique.

Structural Notes

> Walk around your home to determine the flow of your party. Scout out the site of your various stations.

> The location of your stations will determine the flow of your party. The goal is to provide areas where people can congregate and mingle. Guests should be able to flow effortlessly from one station to another and help themselves at the various stations:

   1. Rose Bar/Welcome Station stars the Signature Cocktail and French Beaujolais Wine.

   2. The Main Dining Buffet displays all the fabulous finger foods, so select a spot that guests can easily access and maneuver with a glass and plate in hand.

   3. The Dessert Cart likewise offers a treat for your guests as it presents an array of mini-desserts served on white Chinese soup spoons. The effect of the white Chinese soup spoons en masse is impressive, so give this area some distinction and select a spot that allows easy access and maneuvering.

   4. The Shopping Area: Work with an "in-home" sales representative to select a space conducive to displaying products for easy and fun shopping.

> It is always considerate to provide several small seating areas for your guests to relax and truly enjoy the vibe of the party. Create "vignettes" by grouping pillows, benches, stools, and small chairs around existing seating areas/cocktail table(s). Make sure your vignettes can seat at least three or four people.

Tablescape

THE WHAT A GIRL WANTS TABLESCAPE needs to be pretty in pink! Therefore, bright pink roses are essential; couple them with Green Cymbidium Orchids to create a simple and stately arrangement that speaks to the heart of every woman. Mirrors, candles, and touches of gold finish a look that is simple, elegant, and as devastatingly beautiful as you and your guests. These are the perfect "accessories" to enhance your buffet of fancy finger foods: Apple and Brie Crostini, Potato Nests with Sour Cream and Toppings, Belgian Endive BLT, Tartlettes with Roasted Red Pepper and Goat Cheese, and Roast Beef Croustades with Horseradish.

SCALE 1½" = 1 FT.
DRAWN BY:-
TRACED BY:-
CHECKED BY:-
SKETCH SHEET.
DATE

PARTYBLUPRINTS

HOW TO BUILD A TABLESCAPE

1. Inventory Materials

2. Build Foundation

3. Add Structural Elements

4. Decorate

Tablescape Materials List

INCLUDED IN COMPREHENSIVE MATERIALS LIST

MAIN DINING BUFFET: Turn your dining table into a fabulous feminine feast of Fancy Nibbles.

USE THESE MATERIALS TO CREATE YOUR TABLESCAPE:
> Gold/brass containers/dishes for candles
> White pillar candles and votives
> Floral centerpiece
> Mirrors
> Serving pieces (glass, crystal, white)—platters, plates, trays, cake pedestals
> White/clear dishes and napkins
> Fancy Nibbles
> Menu

Structural Notes

1. INVENTORY YOUR MATERIALS

Take your Materials List (included at end of plan), and go on a scavenger hunt in your home. Stick with a clear glass/crystal, white, and gold/brass palette for your foundation items (serving pieces, candlesticks, dishes, etc.), and don't forget your vintage stuff. Select a "staging" area near your table. Deposit all items you have collected there. Then, "play" with the items and arrange them until you've built your tablescape. Store unused items.

2. BUILD FOUNDATION

Use either your bare wood/glass table or cover with a white tablecloth.

3. ADD STRUCTURAL ELEMENTS

Use a floral arrangement as your centerpiece flanked by white candles on either side.

Floral centerpiece | Hot pink roses and Green Cymbidium Orchids are the perfect balance of sophisticated elegance and sheer fun. When you look at these colors, you can't help but feel lively and happy. *BUILDER'S NOTE:* **How to DIY:** *Fill a clear glass cylinder vase with water and line inside of vase with Thai leaf (or other large green leaf), cut stems of roses and orchids so they rest slightly above the top of vase, tightly gather roses and orchids (mix together flowers for assorted color) and insert bouquet in vase; make slight arrangements as necessary.* **DIY Alternative:** *Order from local florist.*

Mirror | Place in the middle of your table, using it to anchor your floral arrangement and two flanking pillar candles set upon gold/brass plates.

Menu | Place copy in a pretty frame, and prominently display it so your guests can be informed on the selections.

Candles | Use candles of different heights: pillars, votives, candelabras and candlesticks. Keep the candles scentless and the same color; we suggest white. Don't place candles near edge of table or in direct path of guests' reach.

4. DECORATE

Serving pieces | Arrange your serving platters, plates, trays, etc., for your Fancy Nibbles. Put your own personal touch on displaying all your Fancy Nibbles. Consider the size, material, and height of your serving pieces when planning the layout. Treat your table like a display case and give each fancy nibble its own area of distinction. Since the fare is all finger food, you don't need any silverware. Simply stack your plates (use basic white dishes or clear glass plates) on one end of the table with napkins to allow guests to serve themselves buffet style. Serving the ladies in this fashion will encourage your guests to make a plate and eat when they want as opposed to being interrupted all evening with passed or intermittently served appetizers. This format for the evening is conducive to any type of event, e.g., shopping, demonstration, speaker, discussion, and/or socializing!

Fancy Nibbles | Before guests arrive, display all the plated appetizers (see Structural Notes in Food section for tips on displaying appetizers) on Main Dining Table so guests can make "big 'small' plates." Making an entrée out of appetizers is the perfect way for girls to eat! You get a variety of tastes and are not loaded down with a heavy meal. Since everything is a pretty bite-size nibble, there is no need for forks or knives. Guests can take their plate for a spin while perusing the merchandise you have displayed in your in-home boutique.

THE DESSERT CART

Create a fantastic display of delicious desserts with Chinese soup spoons. *Partybluprints Pick: White Chinese porcelain soup spoons may be found in a kitchen supply store or online.*

Materials

Six-foot table(s)
White tablecloth(s)
40 mini desserts served on white Chinese soup spoons
Large mirror
Multitude of candles
Gold/brass dishes for pillar candles
Bright pink rose petals
Optional: Hot pink topper tablecloth

Structural Notes

> Drape six-foot table with a white tablecloth. If you have another large table (in addition to dining room table) you can use that as the foundation for your dessert display—you may opt to leave it bare if it is wood or glass as opposed to covering with white tablecloth. If you have the space, use two six-foot tables for additional impact.
  Optional: Top surface with a hot pink topper tablecloth for added contrast.

> Use a large mirror as an anchor in the center of the table. Depending on the size of your mirror, use it to create a centerpiece of candles using a collection of white pillar candles varying in height and resting on gold/brass plates. If it is a really large mirror, you have the option to display the soup spoon desserts on the mirror. If you do not have a topper, sprinkle hot pink rose petals all over the table like a bed of roses.

> Arrange the prepared dessert spoons in either two large cascading arches or in an array (rows and columns), Strawberry and Chocolate Spoonfuls on one side and the Double Chocolate Brownie Bites on the other. Make sure that all the handles of the soup spoons are arranged in the same direction along each arc. Set up this scrumptious bar before the party starts. As the evening proceeds, casually invite guests to enjoy this area. This station should be in an area away from the shopping. Invite your guests to partake in the menu in any order they choose. Remember, this party is about what a girl wants and when she wants it.

BUILDER'S NOTE: See Structural Notes in Cocktail section for instructions on setting up your beverages at the Rose Bar. Here are notes on creating small satellite flower arrangements for other areas of your party. Use your special touch to create and determine where your "footprint" needs an extra pop of color.

ROSE VOTIVES are the perfect petite arrangements to enhance your party. We used them at the Rose Bar, but you can place them anywhere you choose. They are compact but striking and can be displayed as a trio or individually throughout the party. Here's how to create:
1) DIY: Use a plain rocks glass as your vase, fill with water and line inside of vase with a Thai Leaf (or other large green leaf), if necessary cut width of leaf to fit height of glass. Cut stems of roses to height of glass. Tightly gather roses and arrange in vase so the bottom of the flowers skim top of vase. **2) DIY alternative**: Order from local florist.

BUILDER'S NOTE: If your glass is on the small side and your roses are large, you may only need one large hot pink rose/arrangement.

Architect's Notes
INSIDER'S TIPS

1 **Choose an established and reputable company** to feature at your party—one you are excited to introduce to your guests. Make sure you set the correct tone for your guests; this isn't an obligation to buy, it's simply an opportunity to experience a new product line.

2 **When you are conducting** your selection process for a sales representative, ask if they are willing to donate a portion of the night's sales to a charitable organization of your choosing.

3 **Remind the girls** that this is a great opportunity to have a Ladies' Night Out and do some gift buying. Encourage guests to think of upcoming birthdays, anniversaries or other special occasions/holidays when considering purchases.

4 **Meet with the sales representative** before your party to discuss logistics. A professional will know how to display the products best, but you need to agree on where this should be in your home. The representative may require ample space for displaying products, so dedicate enough room for the girls to shop without being crowded.

5 **If the sales representative** needs to have access to a phone jack/outlet for customer checkout, consider this in your set up. You want your guests to have a positive purchasing experience.

6 **If your living space** is at a premium, display your products vertically in addition to horizontally. Use available shelving, pedestals, and tiered stands to go up instead of out—be creative and have some fun with your display. Other great spots to display product: fireplace hearth, mantle, bar, and cocktail table.

7 **Make sure your boutique** is well lit so your guests can get a good look at the merchandise. You may even want to bring in an extra lamp or two.

8 **You will need a lot of glasses,** including a champagne flute and wine glass for each guest. They do not need to match, so feel free to borrow what you need. If you are hosting a really large crowd for your party, renting is a great option and many rental companies pick up the dirty glasses the next day. This is really what a girl wants!

9 **Pay attention to the powder room** for this What a Girl Wants party. Ladies like to be pampered, so put out some pretty soaps, hand cream, and

disposable hand towels. If your featured product line is skin-care based, feature an item (hand lotion or soap) in your powder room. If you have supply and space, include a rose votive in your powder room.

10 Invite gal pals from different areas of your life: work, school, home, etc. Let this be an opportunity for your friends to make new friends. Hosting a party is about making connections with those you love, so spread the love.

11 As an added indulgence for yourself, hire a bartender. This optional element adds an unexpected layer of sophistication and elegance to the evening.

12 Remember the "U" in Partybluprints and add your special touches. Bring your "builder's inspiration" to your party by sharing with your "girls" your favorite products and charity and adding some of your favorite songs that fit the vibe into the music mix.

Materials List

USE THE INCLUDED MATERIALS LIST as your inventory and shopping list all in one. Simply make a copy and check off items you have before doing any shopping. Then, as you shop, continue to inventory items until all materials are "in-house."

Be efficient and keep an updated copy of your list with you whenever you go shopping and update it in real time. This avoids over purchasing and last minute impulse shopping (we like to call it "panic purchasing"), resulting in unnecessary stress and expenditures.

Critical Path

FOLLOW THE INCLUDED CRITICAL PATH to manage your time and tasks so you are not overwhelmed or unprepared for your guests. This guide combines your to-do list and timeline for efficient and effective preparation and execution. We've removed the guesswork and streamlined the process. If you stick to the Party Plan, you can prepare everything ahead of time and be a guest at your own party. What a sweet reward for a job well done!

PARTYBLUPRINTS WHAT A GIRL WANTS
MATERIALS LIST
SHOPPING LIST FOR 20

- [ ] 7 bottles Brut Rosé Sparkling Wine
- [ ] 40 edible crystallized sweetheart roses
- [ ] 10 bottles Beaujolais
- [ ] 3 six-packs seltzer/club soda
- [ ] 3 six-packs Diet Coke/Sprite
- [ ] 1 (32 oz.) container pomegranate juice
- [ ] 3 limes
- [ ] 2 (16 oz.) containers strawberries
- [ ] 2 large French baguettes
- [ ] ½ cup olive oil
- [ ] kosher salt/coarse sea salt
- [ ] fresh cracked pepper
- [ ] 2 Granny Smith apples
- [ ] 1 cup lemon juice
- [ ] 1 (2 lb.) Brie wheel
- [ ] 1 (11 oz.) container walnuts
- [ ] 2 (30 oz.) bags frozen shredded hash brown potatoes
- [ ] 1 large onion
- [ ] 7 large eggs
- [ ] 2 cups sour cream
- [ ] $^1/_3$ cup fresh sliced chives
- [ ] 1 oz. caviar (optional)
- [ ] 60 Belgian endive spears (approximately 6 heads of endive)
- [ ] 12 plum tomatoes
- [ ] 4 lbs. bacon
- [ ] 4 small to medium round red tomatoes (need for presentation so pick the best looking)

- [ ] 3 Tbsp. mayonnaise
- [ ] 1 box garlic croutons
- [ ] 3 packages mini fillo shells (15/Box)
- [ ] 2 (4 oz.) logs plain goat cheese
- [ ] 1 (12 oz.) container roasted red peppers
- [ ] 2 loaves sliced white bread
- [ ] ½ stick butter
- [ ] 1 lb. very thinly sliced rare deli roast beef
- [ ] 1 cup fresh horseradish
- [ ] 1 bunch fresh Italian parsley
- [ ] 1 jar chocolate sauce
- [ ] 20 long-stemmed strawberries
- [ ] 1 box brownie mix (double chocolate or chocolate chunk variety)
- [ ] $^1/_3$ cup vegetable oil (may need to adjust amount to your brownie mix's instructions)
- [ ] 2 containers fresh raspberries
- [ ] 1 bunch fresh mint
- [ ] 1 lb. coffee
- [ ] cream
- [ ] sugar
- [ ] favor materials (cookies and packaging)
- [ ] 20 champagne flutes
- [ ] 20 red wine glasses
- [ ] 20 water glasses
- [ ] 1 or 2 large glass pitcher(s)/beverage dispenser

PARTYBLUPRINTS WHAT A GIRL WANTS
MATERIALS LIST
SHOPPING LIST FOR 20

- ☐ 4 dozen hot pink roses
- ☐ 3 stems Green Cymbidium Orchids
- ☐ Thai leaves
- ☐ 1 clear glass medium-cylinder vase
- ☐ 3 or more small glass cylinder vases (they look like plain rocks/juice glasses)
- ☐ 2 white pillar candles (same size)
- ☐ assorted white pillar candles
- ☐ gold/brass plates for pillar candles

- ☐ 20 white/clear glass dishes
- ☐ 40 cocktail napkins
- ☐ 40 Chinese white soup spoons
- ☐ Assorted glass/clear/white serving dishes/bowls and serving utensils
- ☐ large mirror
- ☐ smaller mirror (optional)
- ☐ hot pink topper tablecloth (optional)
- ☐ 1 or 2 six-foot tables (white tablecloths to match)

NOTES

....

....

....

....

....

....

....

....

....

....

....

PARTYBLUPRINTS WHAT A GIRL WANTS
CRITICAL PATH
TIMELINE/TO-DO LIST

Requires Immediate Attention (at least three weeks in advance)

☐ Choose the date for your Partybluprints What a Girl Wants Party.

☐ Select a product and contact a sales representative. Schedule and meet in your home to discuss logistics for the evening and view samples of the product(s).

☐ Create a guest list.

☐ Send out invitations.

☐ Determine which items you have in stock (accessories, tableware, serving pieces, tools, tables, tablecloths).

☐ Order items you need well in advance of your party. (See Materials List.)

The Week before the Party

☐ Inventory items for the party and purchase any products still needed.

☐ Test your music sound system and create your playlist/burn CD.

☐ If ordering flower arrangements, order and schedule delivery date of the day before your party. Otherwise, order flowers and DIY.

One to Two Days before the Party

☐ Shop for any last minute items, e.g., fresh produce, meats, cheeses, flowers.

☐ Make the croustades, cool, and store in an airtight container. (Don't fill with roast beef until right before serving.)

☐ Bake Brownie Bites, cool, store in airtight container, and freeze.

☐ Bake cookies, frost, and store in airtight container.

☐ Print out the Menu included in this Partybluprints Party Plan, frame it and display it.

One Day before the Party

☐ Take some time to choose an outfit in which you look and feel fantastic!

☐ If you did not order flower arrangements, create flower arrangements.

☐ Chop roasted red peppers.

☐ Chop onion for potato nests.

☐ Put frozen shredded potato in refrigerator to thaw.

☐ Cook and crumble bacon.

☐ Prepare crostini, cool and store in airtight container (don't top—just prepare crostini portion).

☐ Arrange edible crystallized sweetheart roses in container.

☐ Package favors.

☐ Chill the sparkling wine and non-alcoholic beverages.

☐ Make sure tablecloth(s) are stain free, clean and ironed.

- ☐ Set up Welcome Station/Rose Bar, Main Dining Buffet, and the Dessert Cart with tablecloths, mirrors, candles, flowers, and serving pieces.

Day of the Party

- ☐ Start the day off on a good note; it's the day of your party!
- ☐ Designate a time to get yourself ready and stick to it.
- ☐ Have a cup of coffee or whatever gets you going and start the final preparations for your party!
- ☐ Remove Brownie Bites from freezer, thaw, and follow serving directions.
- ☐ Rinse Belgian endive, dry extremely well, and refrigerate.
- ☐ Dice tomatoes.
- ☐ Prepare Potato Nests, cool, and cover.
- ☐ Set up coffee station and favors.
- ☐ Test the music system.

Three Hours before the Party

- ☐ Mix BLT mixture, stuff endive spears, arrange on platters, cover and refrigerate. (Arrange remaining ingredients on another platter, cover, and refrigerate.)
- ☐ Remember the "U" in Partybluprints and add your special touches, if you haven't already.
- ☐ You followed the Partybluprints Party Plan and physically prepared the party, now it's time to prepare you. Shower and dress in something that makes you feel great. Let the excitement of your party envelop you.

Two Hours before the Party

- ☐ Wash and dry raspberries and strawberries.
- ☐ Prepare Strawberries and Chocolate Spoonfuls, arrange on Dessert Cart.
- ☐ Prepare Double Chocolate Brownie Bites, arrange on Dessert Cart.

One Hour before the Party

- ☐ Prepare Tartlettes, arrange on serving pieces, and display on Main Dining Buffet.
- ☐ Cut apples, bathe in lemon juice.
- ☐ Warm Brie.
- ☐ Prepare Apple and Brie Crostini, arrange on serving pieces, and display on Main Dining Buffet.
- ☐ Prepare Potato Nests and Toppings, arrange on serving pieces, and display on Main Dining Buffet.
- ☐ Prepare Roast Beef Croustades, arrange on serving pieces and display on Main Dining Buffet.

Thirty Minutes before the Party

- ☐ Remove Belgian Endive BLTs from refrigerator and display on Main Dining Buffet.
- ☐ Fill ice buckets and put sparkling wine on ice.
- ☐ Open a few bottles of French Beaujolais Wine and place them on ice.
- ☐ Light the candles.

Fifteen Minutes before the Party

- ☐ Start the music.
- ☐ Take a walk around, admire your work, and feel the vibe.

☐ Pop the bubbly.

☐ Pour yourself a cocktail and toast yourself for a job well done!

During the Party

☐ Make sure all your guests have a drink.

☐ Re-stock bar and Fancy Nibbles when necessary.

☐ Make the coffee.

☐ Cheers on throwing a fabulous party!

NOTES